ISBN 978-1-5284-7739-0
PIBN 10115059

This book is a reproduction of an important historical work. Forgotten Books uses state-of-the-art technology to digitally reconstruct the work, preserving the original format whilst repairing imperfections present in the aged copy. In rare cases, an imperfection in the original, such as a blemish or missing page, may be replicated in our edition. We do, however, repair the vast majority of imperfections successfully; any imperfections that remain are intentionally left to preserve the state of such historical works.

OTHER POEMS

BY

CHARLES DE KAY

33

NEW YORK
CHARLES SCRIBNER'S SONS
1880

POEMS OUT OF TOWN.

PEACE.

KEEN gleams the wind, and all the ground
  Is bare and chapped with bitter cold.
The ruts are iron; fish are found
  Encased in ice as in a mold;
The frozen hilltops ache with pain
  And shudders tremble down each shy
Deep rootlet burrowing in the plain;—
  Now mark the sky.

Softly she pulls a downy veil
  Before her clear Medusa face;
This, falling slow, abroad doth trail
  Across the wold a feathery trace,
Whereunder soon the moaning earth
  Aslumber stretches dreamily,
Forgot both pain and summer's mirth,
  Soothed by the sky.

SONG.

THE winter woods, the winter woods,
They bevel best with all our moods,
   With hardihood and wild despair,
With tender love and joyousness:
The crimes of cities they redress,
   And broken faiths repair.

The winter woods, the winter woods
Are better far than house and goods,
   Than food and raiment better far,
Than gilded walls and canopies:
They break but do not stop the breeze,
   And never hide a star.

The winter woods, the winter woods,
All graces lurk within their buds;
   With melodies in branches fanned
A lofty dance they indicate;
All bookish craft they subtly state,
   With colors fill the land.

Song.

The winter woods, the winter woods
Are loveliest ere the April floods,
   In naked swaying grandeur seen,
Before they know the name of blame,
Before the May cries, Hide for shame
   Your charms in robes of green!

WITH LIFE—HOPE.

NOT a breath!
How a master-wizard's hand
Has to perfect stillness banned
Every snow-heaped minaret
Of the cedars thickly set!
Yonder grasses
Down the passes
Feel a spell that's neither life nor death.

Then the sky!
All the misty webs are brushed
Into solid cloud-rows, crushed
'Gainst the stony blue in ranks:
Sun and wind upon those banks,
Nowise haunted,
Yet enchanted,
Vainly force or blandishments would try.

With Life—Hope.

But this leaf?
Near it nothing life betrays,
Yet alive on branch it sways,
Sere and merry.   Still to go
After comrades 'neath the snow
Is it trying?
What from dying
Keeps a thing of summer-life so brief?

Ah, behold!
What is snugly woven up
In the oak-leaf's crumpled cup?
Cradled warm in gray cocoon
Lies a lady moth: in June,
With the swallow
From her hollow
Leaf outsprung, to flit o'er wood and wold.

SONG FOR WINTER.

ACROSS the ice, across the ice
On wood and steel we sink and rise,
Approach, recede and whirl about,
Engrave initials in and out;
Then he who tries a wintry cooing
Will quickly find a mischief brewing,
For she will fly and he must follow
Where the ice is false and hollow;
She'll lead him heavy and blind and slow
Over the tickly-benders O !

Over the snow, over the snow
On steel and wood and furs we go!
The sleigh-bell merrily madly chinks
And harness in the moonlight blinks;
Cheeks are rosy, eyes are bright,
Cupid's frosty bow has might;
Two shoes under the furs must keep
Two shoes warm and free from sleep;

Words are saucy, breath is sweet,
Comes a bump—and lips will meet!

Around the coals, around the coals
In circle pass the steaming bowls.
We sing and gossip half the night,
As if the niggard sun to spite.
The sailor yarns ; the traveler lies ;
We swallow hard, and wink our eyes.
When stories take the wits to task
The key to doubt is in the flask.
We drink confusion to the snow
And laugh to hear the north winds blow.

Deep down in bed, deep down in bed
We burrow snug when all's been said :
One genial moment list the gale
Against the windows dash the hail,
The next, swim out on tides of dream
Where things outlandish usual seem.
But here's the face we love and cherish,
The heavenly soul for whom we perish !
Blissful we wake :—and white and warm
We clasp the pillow in our arm !

ODE TO WINTER.

SOVEREIGN of my heart, how glorious is thy splendor,
  How thy face of snowplains veined with azure
    streams,
Eyes of lakes o'erfrozen, are radiant yet untender—
  Tresses brown of woodlands—glance of cool sun-
    beams!
When the north wind chideth, how rings out thy
    laughter;
  When the south wind pleadeth, how unstirred thy
    heart;
In thy strength defying all that cometh after,
  Child in form of goddess, unconquerable thou art!
      Is there naught can take from thee
      Thy too brave prosperity?

What though glad the thoughtless: still is loving
    better
  Than an empty spending of selfish days and free.
Who shall curb thy freedom; who, a blooming fetter
  Lay about thy deep soul, if soul there be to thee?

Underneath the snow-drifts down the woody hollow
Ferns are green and mosses wait a coming word,
Frogs below the wood ponds, and mayhap the swal-
low,
Dream they hear the whistling of a summer bird;
Only thou dost nowise care
What the fiery Spring may dare.

Laurel for that master, apple blooms and roses,
Who can teach the lesson winter will not learn!
Winter, I implore thee, list when he discloses
Hopes of early spring-tide, tells how leaflets yearn,
Grasses seek the sunlight, birds their mates discover,
How the world is action, life and budding change;
Winter, bright and terrible, hear thine ardent lover;
Stand aloof no longer dread and hard and strange!
Melt, O winter; fear no harm
Happed within thy lover's arm!

THE WINTRY ALPHABET.

UPON a sunbaked southern plain
  And through old jungles ever blooming
What shapes would human hands retain
On even surface to explain
  The thoughts that in the mind were looming?

Nor plain was marked, nor mount, nor wood;
  These looked unchanged the heavens under,
But bulls that charged and huts that stood
And deer on hill and fish in flood—
  They roused man's wish and wonder.

And so, their figures daubed on bark,
  On hides, on mud bricks, formed his data,
And through the æons we call dark
He fanned with hieroglyphs the spark
  Of learning to an alphabeta.

Not so the Northman.   Half his year
  He mused on one of Nature's pages,
And watched, untouched his bow and spear,
Through the wide gleaming snows uprear
  Their heads these letters, dumb for ages.

On yonder sloping crest of hill
  Behold the bare elms, oaks and birches:
Each tree's a letter cut with skill,
Sharp-edged, a text for good or ill,
  A script not hid when wisdom searches.

The tree trunks, how they leap from snow!
  Each several crown, what free resplendence!
Some day like this a bard aglow
With nervous forethought notched them slow
  To runes—and awed his rude descendants.

THE LAST PINE.

WHERE the fallow-colored hill
   Juts against a cloudy wreath—
   Gray the sky, the ground beneath
White with shreds from winter's quill—

Holds a pine of giant girth
   All alone a patience grim
   In the ghastly cold, the dim
Sifted light that wraps the earth;

Like a soldier strictly charged
   Never from his watch to yield:
   Long ago was hushed the field,
All his comrades, long discharged:

Solid hangs the icy tear,
   Numb his arms with creeping frost,
   And his senses four are lost
In a bitter strife to hear:

Yet unmoved he keepeth post,
　Dim of sight but list'ning still,
　Lest across the lonely hill
Call the bugles of the host!

Once upon a silent day
　Heaved the tree such breath profound,
　Air was carded into sound,
Thus the pine was heard to say:

　　" One by one,
Though they towered high and wide,
Sank my brothers by my side,
Fell away my friends of youth :
Death on them had never ruth.
　　One by one
Dropped my warming arms of green
Till I stand of branches lean ;
Straight the woodpecker may shoot
From my crown to knotted root :
　　All is done !

I am past.
Once I dwelt with fellows dear,
Once I felt the green sod near ;
Year by year
In the choir of our wood
Crashed a singer where he stood,
And the boughs that rained forever,
Lowest first then upward ever
On his bier,
Me with their wide loss did sever
Still the more from things I love
Into this drear air above.

I might last
Happy, if my shadow cast
One deep roof of solid cool
On a wise man, on a fool,
On the lowest shape that passed ;
If the sun, like this harsh air,
Lingered in my scattered hair ;
But no grace from me descends
While I drag to useless ends
Life at last."

THE MOTH.

WHERE for carpet lay the gaunt brown trees below
    Sifted snow,
On a cruel sundown in a losing strife
    Writhed a life;
Quaking pale-brown wings and tender coming breath
    Fought with death.

Frail the moth and weak till warmed by heat of hand;
    Closely scanned
All the horizon showed no garden summer-sweet
    For his feet,
Yet undoubting, from the savior palm upreared,
    Straight he steered

Forthright to his one place in this dual world.
    Winter-hurled,
Fine sleet stung him as he beat the evening late
    Toward his mate
Where, by paths untrod, but O, dreamt of,
    Lay his love.

ROBBER BLUEBACK.

THOUGH it lacks two months of May
    Frosts have nipped a genial thaw
And the melted snow is thin
    Crisp and harsh to Renard's claw.
White are curves where paths have been
    Winding through the ruddy swamp,
Pensive-gray the circling trees
    Etch the sky in gentle pomp.
Yet is spring within the breeze,
    Gay in heart of yonder fowl
Screaming near a brooding owl
        His *jay—jay—jay !*

Wicked dandy, have you come
    Dressed in suit of brightest blue
Long among our hills to roam
    Till the woods your presence rue?
Malice sure your notes betray
While you flirt about each gray

Brushy top and chestnut crest
Jotting down in thievish brain
Just the lay of every nest;
So, when summer's here again—
Suck the eggs—away you fly
With the parent-frighting cry
Of *jay—jay—jay !*

Ah the dainty rascal jay!
Now's the time abroad to fling
With the heart and limbs of youth
Ere the fickle minded spring
All the land with lakes endu'th!
Now across the oak-swamp race
Following swift his airy trace;
Hound him down the icy path
Till he chatters full of wrath;
Chase him past the helpless owl
And loudly mock the coward fowl
With *jay—jay—jay !*

SONG FOR SPRING.

LILAC clouds and purple tinted branches,
  Solid blues within the wintry sky,
Tawny browns o'er windy desolate marshes,
  Gleams that blind where ice and snow-banks lie!
See, the violets call from out the grasses,
  Look, the purple answers from the ground;
Azure melts and to that warbler passes,
  Sudden, a skyfleck on the fences found!
                The turning year
                Is here, here, here,

        Daily the joyous hilltops run
            Nearer, more near
      To your high seat, O golden glorious sun!

Angry winds that clashed their airy pinions
  Round the homestead prune dead leaves away;
Rains that stung when they were sleet or snowflake
  Ease the buds that lurk below the clay;

For they know the one great god is coming,
  Lord of all, whose hair disparteth gloom.
List to the south—his herald bees are humming!
  Lo, how his brow reddens the ocean spume!
        His heart so hot
        Has altered naught,
    Now that the year around hath spun
        All hail be brought
    To you, the god and giver of life, O sun!

Soon the molten gold that brings no sadness
  Thick shall lie on pasture land and moor;
Soon the broad unstinted sun shall gladden
  Gates of rich men, hovels of the poor:
Bat-wing'd moths, in boles of trees entombéd,
  Feel the root-blood through the twigs aspire,
Stir impatient, sure their pinions humid
  Soon shall dry before the all-fostering fire.
        That Lord so good
        orgets no bud,
    'Tis you, you, you whose charm has won
        From yonder sod
    To heaven that high and branching oak, O
    sun!

Birds by thousand far off groves are wending
 Northward still their solitary way;
Soon their mates will find them in each forest,
 Field or marsh while yet the woods are gray.
Hear them laugh in liquid notes and cooing,
 Watch them sail in airiest curving flight,
'Tis but earth the wondrous sun god wooing,
 'Tis the darkness yearning for the light!
     Wake to their voice
     And take your choice,
 Ye men and maidens every one;
     Rejoice, rejoice
 With you, O gold-cored lover of earth, great
     sun!

WOOD LAUREL.

WHITE in coverts of the wood
Where the even shadows brood,
On waving carpets young of fern
See the clusters steadfast burn,— ·
Eyes of joy amid the dark
Lighting up the forest stark!
While the pine is bending over,
Tenderly, a rugged lover,
Thankful faces we must wear
Since the laurel blooms so fair.

At what altar shall we pray?
For his neighbor who shall say?
Each devout may draw his moral
For the generous blooming laurel.
Let the priest of gods triune
List to Nature's triple rune,
Symbols find in leaf and petal
Which no councils can unsettle,

Giving praise as well as prayer
That the laurel blooms so fair.

Here the lover of one God
One law reads in oak and sod;
Swedenborg's etherial sons
May see the woodsprite for the nonce,
And Moslem who toward Mecca yearns
May spread his carpet 'mid the ferns
And watching with adoring eyes
These petals tint with pink sunrise,
May lift to Allah thankful prayer
That the laurel blooms so fair.

Buddhist here can fix his gaze
Where encounter beauty's rays,
In this lovely foam discern
Sign of Nature's yeasty churn;
And China's wise and formal seer
Beholds the perfect symbol here
Of work and work's consummate fruit
In flower, in bush and groping root.
These a moment more may spare
Since the laurel blooms so fair.

Laurel once was victor's weed,
This one's not of warlike breed;
Blooming, lost in forest dense,
With a shy luxuriance,
She is glad to be the bush
Favored by the brown-winged thrush,
Loving more his melting song
Than the plaudits of the throng;—
O, that I the woods might share
Which the laurel makes so fair!

TO SILVER LAKE.

Ah, little lake where the sleepy cows
   Rest in the autumn night,
Rest under high fantastic boughs
    Of the oak, slant gleams of white!
      Till your springs run dry
      You may smile on the sky,
You may pout and storm and bluster,
      May whisper with reed
      And in dark heart breed
Deep lily-pad secrets acluster.

But oh, little lake, when man, the ant,
   Gnaws at your flowery brink,
Your soul will fail, your pride grow scant,
    Your cows low in vain for drink;
      With dim tortured eyes
      You will beg of the skies
For rain as thick as a river,
      Or else that a quake
      The hard earth break
And drain you at once and forever.

ON GREAT SOUTH BAY.

O, HERE behind that rosary emerald-gray
   Whose brown and opal beads are mounds of sand,
To cut and cut the turquoise of the bay,
   Yet feel the greater paths beyond the land. . .

O, held from death by boards a shaving thick
   And by the pleasure of a fair wind blowing,
Or snatched at by the spray-hand of each quick
   Relentless wave forever by me flowing. . .

Day after day to toil behind that veil. . .
   The tiny ring-neck hid by dazzling shore
Turned, ages past, his piping to a wail
   To pierce, sad, constant, through the breaker's roar.

Out, out beyond these long dun sandy coils
   Beckons this morn a red heart of surprise
Just where the fog-veil, sliding ruddy, foils
   A shape within the tragic-deep sunrise

Which, voiceless, speaks: " Why drag ye empty hours
  Until, the last locked bay and farthest strait
Passed, the inevitable ocean lowers
  Dark to faint heart that leaves all till too late?"

Ay, why vain shallows, adverse currents small
  Of duty try, when these light cockles, thus
With strong soul dashed against the breaker-wall,
  May ride, or broken, may give life to us?

Home—country—friends? What hollow words at
    best
  Which drench not souls with bliss as doth the roar
From giant pipes of color far to west—
  Dumb, dumb to human ears forevermore.

THE WHIPPOORWILL.

WHIPPOORWILL, *whippoorwill, whippoorwill!*
How I hate your frenzied note
Stinging like a driver's switch
Through the midnight black as pitch!
Evil sights have you to show:
Wearied, anxious, crazed with woe,
A woman into madness driven
By crimes unheard-of unforgiven
Is striving with a shapeless throat
For words that make the blood stand still.

Whippoorwill, whippoorwill, whippoorwill!
Ah, the awful nights! Your cry
Seared the brain as drops of lead
Seared the living and the dead
In the days of death, when Grant,
Firm of soul as adamant,
Hurled his luckless regiments
On the rebels' firm defense.

Bird malignant, well may I
Shudder at your moanings shrill!

Whippoorwill, whippoorwill, whippoorwill!
Bird that horrors must rehearse,
How you told the seconds through
(Hours of anguish, years of rue!)
When, before the earthworks lying,
Men were killed without replying;
When each moment through the black
Sprang a flash!—a rifle's crack—
A groan—on you a dying curse—
And one more valiant heart was still!

Whippoorwill, whippoorwill, whippoorwill!
Desolate wailer of the night,
Be henceforward you to men
Sign of murder, fever, pain
And symbol of that ashen star
Which rules the hell of civil war.
But souls hereafter, sensitive,
Shall list you moan and deeply grieve,
Shall tremble at a nation's plight
And dream that wrong the right shall kill.

Whippoorwill, whippoorwill, whippoorwill!
Here where slaves have laughed and sighed,
Loathed their chains and loved them too,
In one note condensed by you
All the sadness of their laughter,
All their anguish shall hereafter
Pour in ceaseless woe and blind
A wordless tale of men unkind!
Through boundless light shall eagles ride;
Yours be the tangle past the hill.

RICHMOND, Va.

THE TORNADO.

WHOSE eye has marked his gendering? On his
    throne
He dwells apart in roofless caves of air,
Born of the stagnant, blown of the glassy heat
O'er the still mere Sargasso. When the world
Has fallen voluptuous, and the isles are grown
So bold they cry, God sees not !—as a rare
Sunflashing iceberg towers on high, and fleet
As air-ships rise, by upward currents whirled,
Even so the bane of lustful islanders
Wings him aloft. And scarce a pinion stirs.

There gathering hues, he stoopeth down again,
Down from the vault. Locks of the gold-tipped cloud
Fly o'er his head; his eyes, Saint Elmo flames;
His mouth, a surf on a red coral reef.
Embroidered is his cloak of dark blue stain
With lightning jags. Upon his pathway crowd
Dull Shudder, wan-faced Quaking, Ghastly-dreams.
And after these, in order near their chief,

Start, Tremor, Faint-heart, Panic and Affray,
Horror with blanching eyes, and limp Dismay

Unroll a gray-green carpet him before
Swathed in thick foam: thereon adventuring, bark
Need never hope to live; that yeasty pile
Bears her no longer; to the mast-head plunged
She writhes and groans, careens, and is no more.
Now, prickt by fear, the man-devourer shark,
Gale-breasting gull and whale that dreams no guile
Till the sharp steel quite to the life has lunged,
Before his pitiless, onward-hurling form
Hurry toward land for shelter from the storm.

In vain.   Tornado and his pursuivants,
Whirlwind of giant bulk, and Water-spout,—
The gruesome, tortuous devil-fish of rain,—
O'ertake them on the shoals and leave them dead.
Doomsday has come.   Now men in speechless trance
Glower unmoved upon the hideous rout,
Or, shrieking, fly to holes, or yet complain
One moment to that lordly face of dread
Before he quits the mountain of his wave
And strews for all impartially their grave.

2*

And as in court-yard corners on the wind
Sweep the loose straws, houses and stately trees
Whirl in a vortex.   His unswerving tread
Winnows the isle bare as a thresher's floor.
His eyes are fixed ; he looks not once behind,
But at his back fall silence and the breeze.
Scarce is he come, the lovely wraith is sped.
Ashamed the lightning shuts its purple door,
And heaven still knows the robes of gold and dun,
While placid Ruin gently greets the sun.

ARCANA SYLVARUM.

HARK! . . .
What booming
Faints on the high-strung ear?
Through the damp woods (so dark
No flowers are blooming)
I hear, I hear
The twang of harps, the leap
Of hairy feet, and know the revel's ripe,
While, like a coral stripe,
The lizard cool doth creep,
Monster, but monarch there, up the pale Indian Pipe.

Hush! . . .
Your panting
Will scare them from their game.
Let not a foot-fall crush
Their rites enchanting!
The deadwood's flame,
Bellies of murdered fire-flies,

And glimmering moonstones thick with treasured rays
Shall help our round-eyed gaze
Antics unholy to surprise
Which the ungodly crew round the red lizard plays.

Now ! . . .
No breathing
To spoil the heathenish dance !
Lest from each pendent bough
Poison be seething,—
A hair-fine lance
Pierce to our brain, and slowly slay.
But look your breathless fill, and mark them swing,
Man and maid a-capering,
Ugly, fair, morosely gay,
Round the red lizard smooth, crowned for their
    wicked king.

Back ! . . .
Inhuman
Are gestures, laughs, and jeers.
Off, ere we lose the track !
Nor man, nor woman
May stand your leers,

Shameless and loose, uncovered creatures!
Quick, lest we join their orgies in the dark!
Back! For the madness stark
Is crawling through our natures
To touch the red lizard vile, spread on the damp
white bark.

ON REVISITING STATEN ISLAND.

AGAIN ye fields, again ye woods and farms
Slowly approach and fold me to your arms.
The scent of June buds wraps me once again,
The breath of grasses sighs along the plain.
Ye elms and oaks that comforted of yore,
I hear your welcome as I heard before;
The night-blue sky is etched with dusky boughs
And at your feet the white and huddled cows
Are breathing deeply still.   Is all a dream,
Or does the hillside with a welcome gleam?
Ye lofty trees, know ye your worshipper?
Know ye a wanderer, ready to aver
Yon branch leans downward to his eager face,
Yon bush seems following on his happy trace!
The cedars gossip softly, one by one,
Leaning their heads in secret; on and on
The whisper spreads, from new-born larch to fir,
Thence to the chestnut tender yet of bur,

And now the fragrant blackberry on the moor
Says the same word the white beech mutters o'er.
A spice-birch on the fringes of the wood
Has lain in wait, has heard and understood ;
The piny phalanx nods, and up, away,
Tree-tops have sped the name to Prince's Bay !

SWALLOW–FLEDGE.

In August, when the lake is low
   And myriad winged things mount the sedge
Themselves on airs unknown to throw,
   Then downy swallowlets are fledge:
With needless haste they veer and sweep
Yet dare not try the greater deep.

About the wavy tops of trees
   They join the weaving parent band,
And since they fear the sportive breeze
   May lilt them high above the land,
They race unsteady to and fro
And chirp for courage as they go.

But high above the yellowing marsh
   And plain against the level sun
The insects rise.   With twitterings harsh
   The elders rush the prey upon:
Then swallowlets with ardor thrill;
The flock has whirled, and the woods are still.

AUTUMN VIEWS.

UNDER the red trees out in the wood
   Yellow are leaves and brown ;
Under the evergreens steadfast of mood
   Ranks of the ruddy are strewn ;
So in this white mist rayed with the gold
      Rugs lie unrolled
  More gorgeous than aught in the town.

Under the gray sky out by the creek
   Yellow are grasses and brown ;
Glassed in a high-tide's silvery streak
   Tall reeds ruddy have grown ;
So by the waters gray gold and green
      Pictures are seen
  More glorious than any in town.

ETERNAL SUMMER.

GOLD of autumn, fairy gold,
  Painting with a separate grace
  Every tree within its place,
Are you fickle as they scold?

Gold of autumn fadeth fast;
  Falls and falls each lingering leaf
  Slanting playful towards the sheaf
Round about the treetrunk cast.

But the treetrunk moulders too;
  All the wood an ocean fills;
  Little rivers gnaw the hills;—
Why should mortals rail at you?

You are stronger than the sea;
  You are longer-lived than hills,
  Since your passing beauty thrills
Souls that haunt eternity.

AUTUMNAL OVERTHROW.

FAREWELL, bright leaves, and softly lie
  In graves below all stormy weather;
  I may not join your fall together
With thoughts forlorn, when lo, I spy
Spread out the gleam and glories mellow
  Of rich brown woods, of lilac shades,
  The purplish hues that fill the glades,
  Each delicate shifting tint that fades
Through all the scale twixt black and yellow.

Bright leaves, till you fell who could mark
  The magic traceries in the thickets?
  A thousand sounds, the shrill of crickets,
The whippoorwill's lost cry, the stark
Black forest shadows, were so valid
  They neutralized each sunborn hue.
  But since from angry steely blue
  The snow on freezing winglets flew—
There lies your background strong and pallid.

Cold sickness, thou with writhen face,
  That camest as from clear air thunder,
  No heart for thee have I, no wonder,
No welcome smile, no word of grace!
And yet, as underneath the trees,
  Before their beauty stood conceded
  A shroud of bitter white was needed—
  Where would our race be now, unweeded
By grisly death and wan disease?

IN AUTUMN.

RED-GOLDEN grass of flames that slowly parch,
Deep umber reeds that burn beside the creek,
O tulip tree, of maiden outline meek,
That yellows clear against the fringe of larch!
Ye purple spaces of the evening bay,
All, all ye shell-rose reaches near the black
Where sleeps the mainland, unseen for the wrack
Of that huge sun which all too soon is gray—
  Speak! for such glories why not worship you?
  Speak! to yourselves is no prostration due?

What! when the moonlight powdereth silver grays
On leaves of maple, ages vast have steeped
In breathless gorgeous sunsets like to-day's—
Whence their thin dyes, fast falling, century heaped,
Have stained small palms uplifted in surprise
At godlike colors—when the moonlight sifts
Silver between the ruddy gold of rifts

In that most royal tree,
    I must not bow the knee!
Must I dam up the pourings of my heart
    For an High God, apart?—
Lo, here I lie and worship ye, wide skies,
For each warm hue that meets these kindling eyes!

SAWS.

WORST of crimes are not of woman:
Horrors halve by being human.

He who sinneth in the city,
May find margin to be witty;

He who in the woods doth sin,
Him the drear fiend enters in.

AT SANDY HOOK.

ALONG the borders of this sterile land
Each wild-beast breaker leaps upon the strand
With such deep mouth that all in fear we stand,

And watch at eve the giant rollers shrink
Before still mightier on the ocean's brink,
And wait by night to feel the whole beach sink

In one wide crash.   At foot full many a shell
Lies deeply hid, and who is he can tell
What marvels may lurk there for him who searcheth
 well?

On yon blue sphere, from spicy islands blown,
What craft shall tooth the rim, spike the unsown
The fruitful field with spars in some strange forest
 grown?

So hand in hand and silent on we stray,
Nor what is waiting in the farther bay,
What the next creek will bring us, who shall say?

For something cometh.   That is wherefore, banned
To salt-soaked beach, with parted lips we stand
And seaward bend our eyes or stare upon the sand.

Each wave is new that mounteth high the shore;
Each cape hath treasures; through the midnight roar,
Hark, surely something comes not seen, not heard
    before!

I. THE WINTER ELF.

DANCE along the new-blown drift,
  Broke the weary chain of things,
Regions wild with hourly shift
  Crag that ne'er a like shade flings!
Whirl across the blackened pond,
  Mock the cranberries through the ice,
Cheeks of me as red and round
  But snow heart and form of ice;
Crystal qualls are likest me
Pulsing through the Arctic Sea.

Shot below the snow-bent pines—
  Holaho, the windy hill!
Down the glorious mad inclines
  Plunging with the tongueless rill!
Tease the white owl while he broods
  Hid within the netted brake
Where, in feathery lace for roods
  Purple lies the solid lake!

Pluck the brittle flower-whorls
   Peeping brown through frosty snow—
Crack from steeps the icy curls,
   Plash them in the brine below!
Sail my ships on crisping seas,
   Hear their white sides clash and groan,
Chase the fog's weird imageries,
   Jeer the north wind's lordly tone!
This is life, this is joyance,
   This pleasure without fault;
Surely thought is but annoyance—
   Only one thing gives me halt:
      There's the moon—!

Some day this shall be my thought
By what will all things are wrought,
If for that bright ball I slave
Stealing from the eastern wave
Spying out each frosty flake
In wood and valley, sea and lake?

Sun has weak uncertain light:
Moon is mighty, strange and bright,
And, though waning waxes fast,

Moves the root of boundless sea,
Stirring that, does moon rule me
    First or last?
    Is this nature mine
    Devil's or divine?
Look, the silly press of mortals,
Toilsome, anxious, blind and tame,
Birth and death a painful name!
Mine is not to pass the portals,
Memory finds me still the same.
Sometimes in the blinding sleet
Swift before a man I fleet
(Heartflake white, a rosy face,
But of body not a trace)
Thinks he dreams; but should I stay
I'm his own god from that day!

God or devil?—Things should bevel,
What is good and what is evil?

Curious human face that striveth
    Grim-set in a bitter death!
When the raving west wind driveth
    Tons of snow on laden breath,

Then upon the prairie group
Lightly from the blast I stoop,
Close the ugly staring eyes,
Smooth the savage glare, arise
  Neither sad,
   No, nor glad ;
Only wonder as I hurry
On the broad back of the skurry
Why men hold relentless strife
For the bubble called a life.

II. SPRING ASKS.

YE knotty roots that roof my bed,
   That frame the valley, arch the pond
   And silver woodslope where, beyond,
Sits a bird on a sumac-head—

You bird on a sun-drugged sumac-head,
   Blue of the back, brown of the breast,
   Who placed you—best?
Was not I last night the child,
   Changeless, mad as leaves that blow
   Playmates mine o'er frosty snow?
Well may south winds blow me mild
       But not change:
Here I wake 'mid flattened leaves
Languid under twisted eaves;
Slim like mortals, shot with strange
Emerald my transparent frame,
   Thin my cheeks and weak my knees—
   Hark, the violet-smoky trees
       Speak my name!

" Up, up, by our hands
   Catch us, savior of the earth,
 Tree and herb at thy commands
   Leap with music into birth,
Spring, Spring, young god Spring— "

Ungainsaid the voices ring,
Every cell o'er night is broken,
All things loss and gain betoken:
Snow from twig and cloud from sky!
Where the ice was broad I spy
Dead gold wavelets; tuneful trees,
Trees majestic march at ease
Down the slope to where I lie—
Hazy masses, dark on dark,
Thick, more thick with budding bark
Till 'mid young brush sweet of smell
     Past the tell,
Flinty edged against the white
Of the snow-banks over night,
Now the shape of gnarring crows
Blurry on the woodside grows.

Work! the stirring branches sing,
  Nor may be denied the chant
  Organ-toned from every plant.
Question comes not, but on wing
  Of the languor-laden air
  Propped, I slide the willow's hair
To the root of fingers lean,
Lo, where'er my touch hath been
Drifts a rain all golden green!
Russet fall the red-oak sheaves,
Maiden beeches drop their leaves—
Tatters thin they chastely drew
Round about when bold winds blew—
And the woods of all the lands
Lift their myriad clenched hands,
Quake—and these from brown gray bands
      Struggle free.

Bird on a storm-beat sumac-head,
Blue o' the back, brown o' the breast,
      I wrought you best!
Or had you otherwise won the red
      Of the sumac-head,

Sweet bird that ever doth blithely wait
For something to come, though it cometh late?
No, you ne'er could hope to guess,
You, nor Sun, though Sun may bless,
Nor the dreadful Moon of night,
Cold and strangely great of might;
       Yes—
God I am; the tangled swamps
Gain from me a thousand new
Wonder-brilliant forms.   The lamps
Borne by myriad wings, the blue
Tender-veined liverwort,
Windflower meek, and coil of fern,
Crocus-flames that have no burn,
These to waken is my sport;
Each of these and all in turn,
Whose deep sleep is danger-fraught,
By my craft to life are brought.
Mottled beak of marshy weed,
Gasping for the air, I feed;
And when great moths, brown and eyed,
Ope their doors, I stand beside;
So from slimy mold I break
Each weak piper by the lake.
   3*

All things alter, burgeon, rise ;
All things veer 'neath changing skies:
Change hath touched me.   Who shall say
Changes come not every day?
I am god, let all things chime.
I am space and I am time.
Only this is past my lore—
What the bird is waiting for?

III. SUMMER ANSWERS.

Love, love—yes, love!
All up the wood the faint aromas creep,
  Sonorous bells are pealing from the lake,
And wide-eyed night is drinking, breathless deep,
  A marsh-born chorus, glorious for the sake
Of some great joy! But we are couched on mould
  Where webs of steep trees etch a mellow moon;
  From rhythmic water pulsing to a tune
Our low lids catch a shifting foil-of-gold:
  For you are found, the riddle, known not of,
  But longed for long—my sun-moon-stars of love.

Mine, mine, ay mine!
At break of day two mortals seen by me,
  Their parting sighs, each warm and clinging breast,
Their reeling eyes that begged yet could not see,
  My smooth joy brake in floes of wild unrest,

Until you came with blue-birds!—whether deep
  In waves you slept, or far in tropic land
  You waked to life on some warm, oozy strand,
Or from my frame were slow shaped in a sleep,
  Or great god Sun, henceforward yours and mine,
  Did lend me you for life's completest sign.

    Ah, rare day—rare!
A hill-close, warm, and brimmed with smell of spring,
  Laid thick with petals apple-orchard strewn
Your feet that day were kissing.   Every wing
  That wafts a bird-voice to your path had flown.
I too, till then by my caprices led,
  So arrowy whirred, swift as a hive-shot bee,
  That close-enlaced, you learnt all things thro' me
Before once turned my way that golden head,
  When, hid by dazzle of your sunshine hairs,
  We kissed, to blush and love all unawares.

    Peace, peace, yea, peace.
The wizard moon shall never chill that breast
  Too rare in charms for mortal maid to own.
These lips shall soothe your broad eyes to a rest
  Neath snowy lids by shadows forest-thrown;

Your tawny frame with languor dewy-sweet
  Pervades my veins, while, folded light and warm,
  Slim limbs of gold-dust with my opal form
In full-blown flowers of spotless passion meet :
  O woods were waiting, nor has thick life ceased
  Its pulsing since, in grass, in bird, in beast.

    Yea, life, life, life !
At my first change the glad earth rustled green ;
  At thy first coming sharper grew the shades,
But now close-linked, the tasseled maize between,
  We guide the hurrying sap, we part the blades
Where thin ears peep ; we fill the buckwheat head,
  And as we pass the peach turns golden-brown ;
  Great roses blow ; the blackberry its crown
Sinks heavily while deeper grows its red.
  O ! love is work ; our life-work, love ; we strive
  In love for new life, and our aims arrive !

    High, fair those aims !
The Sun is god.   'Tis he our being's root
  Blows roundly out to life's perfected sphere.
The glorious sun is mimicked in each fruit,
  But moons are childless, icy-calm, and clear.

When noon gleams hot, and while the rich sap yearns
  Along our veins, we'll broaden our delight
  With help for all that lives, be guard by night
To all fair things within whose fibre burns
  The central sun.   His great will thus he frames
  In two glad slaves, two close-entwinéd flames.

IV. AUTUMN AND FALL.

THIS shall guard you 'gainst the moon,
This, that oft has sheltered you,
   Help-mate true!
See, this arm, that once went round
You, a slender maiden found
   In a June.
Close-linkt then the fields we paced:
Now it may not span your waist.

Let the moon with bitter stare
Walk in haughty state the sky,
   Seem to dry
Sap in tree and juice in grape,
Seem our mighty sun to drape
   With thick air;—
Still the west winds smoothly blow;
Mighty rivers calmly flow.
What if night's breath now be cool,

What, if swallows disappear?
   Do not fear,
Your dear cheeks are full as red
As the ripe leaf overhead!
   By the pool
Lean the red trees strong of heart,
They from life will ne'er depart!

We have done our office well.
Help we gave before we saw
   All the law;
Saw, nor we, nor sun were gods,
That the kindly season plods
   Past our spell;
Yet that earth with joy advances
To our sympathetic dances.

Much we fathomed in our toiling,
Catching many a secret weird
   By the beard
Till its face read plainly.   Often
Harsh things which a touch would soften
   Paid for moiling.
Soon we'll have return for duty
In a child with all your beauty.

Eyes that yearn with deepest sadness,
Dark as gold-cored gentian,
  Why so wan?
Dreamful days portend no sorrow;
From this silent haze we borrow
  Richer gladness;
Hot life grasps the rest it earns,
Quivering, to a still flame burns.

———

When before the giant cold
Through the gateways of the wood
  Runs a shaking;
And red-golden scales are falling
Past the brown and staring limbs;
When the wet leaf prints its mark
  On the mud;
When the trees' black skeletons
  Push in view—
  It is death.

This is death:
All the leaves, red with health,
  All are fallen·:
  So the woman

Once by me loved, now, and always,
　So she passes
From these fields, these mighty forests;
　Yet where she goes
　There go I.

Here upon the ground she lies.
　By her side
Stands an infant icy-cold,
Without heart or brain to know
Whence he comes, who I am—
I, whose minutes all are numbered,
　He, my child!
　For each leaf,
Falling, falling, left behind
　Each a bud:
　So shall we—
She who has but gone before,
I who now am hasting after—
　Live again in him.

　What he is
　Once was I.
Far prophetic vistas open
To my fading eyes.　I reckon

All the days that were and shall be.
He shall never know his parents,
He will sport as once I sported
Through the snowbrush, o'er the mountain,
Careless, free as thistle-down.
Yonder glassy lake that whitens
There, by white sky and by mirror'd
Olive ranks of trees divided
Into semblance of an icecoat,
   Only feigns !—
I shall never see the real sheet
Clear and moveless, yet protecting
Lake and lakefolk from the north winds.
It will be my bold one's play-ground,
There the first-doubt shall assail him
Earlier than assail'd his father—
   Quicker growth
Shall reward his parents' toil.
   Deeper wisdom
   Was engendered
   With his forming !
   We have learned :
Not in vain is any labor
Which for good has been perform'd.

LONGINGS.

A SNAKE with wings, ah would that I might be!
   A coil of curves that, never twice the same,
Still shifts its beauteous links in harmony
   To myriad wreathings of a lissome frame—
A broad-wing'd snake whose vans, when eve is nigh,
May stay the sun by towering up the sky.

What earthly joys to press my yielding form
   To Mother Earth by every hill and hollow!
To flow at noon across the grasses warm,
   And learn the pulses of her heart to follow!
To wind far down the lily-flaked lagoon
And lick cool dews that start beneath the moon!

What joys of air to slide luxurious neck
   O'er smoothest tops of close-enwoven trees!
To touch and taste the sky-swung flowers that deck
   Their loftiest twigs, known to the. dizzy bees!

To ride the waves of russet and of green,
And glide by paths where never man hath been!

So no base thing should hide below my ken
   And no high bird should soar above my sight,
Wild beasts should make me welcome to their den,
   And eagles, that in circles vast delight,
Should wheel with pinions lightly fanning mine
And watch men creep like ants on leaf of vine.

FATE.

NIAGARA, SEPTEMBER, 1879.

THINK you the whirlpool vies under the hard blue skies
    Foaming, tumultuous, with her surrounding steeps?
She, with her mere-green smile deeper than human
    guile
    Sleeps.   She sleeps, sleeps.

Think you the Dragon lies under his purple skies
    Crouched to rush upward from his rock-walled deeps?
Wound in a conscious coil, he of the fated spoil
    Sleeps.   He sleeps, sleeps.

POEMS IN TOWN.

DAWN IN THE CITY.

THE city slowly wakes:
Her every chimney makes
Offering of smoke against the cool white skies.
Slowly the morning shakes
The lingering shadowy flakes
Of night from doors and windows, from the city's eyes.

A breath through heaven goes:
Leaves of the pale sweet rose
Are strewn along the clouds of upper air.
Healer of ancient woes,
The palm of dawn bestows
Peace on the feverish brow, comfort on grim despair.

Now the celestial fire
Fingers the sunken spire,
Crocket by crocket swiftly creepeth down;
Brushes the maze of wire,
Dewy, electric lyre,
And with a silent hymn one moment fills the town.

A sound of pattering hoofs
Above the emergent roofs
And anxious bleatings tell the passing herd;
Scared by the piteous droves,
A shoal of skurrying doves
Veering, around the island of the church has whirred.

Soon through the smoky haze
The park begins to raise
Its outlines clearer into daylit prose;
Ever with fresh amaze
The sleepless fountains praise
Morn that has gilt the city as it gilds the rose.

High in the clearer air
The smoke now builds a stair
Leading to realms no wing of bird has found;
Things are more foul, more fair;
A distant clock somewhere
Strikes, and the dreamer starts at clear reverberant
sound.

Farther the tide of dark
Drains from each square and park:

Here is a city fresh and new-create,
   Wondrous as though the ark
   Should once again disbark
On a remoulded world its safe and joyous freight.

   Ebbs all the dark, and now
   Life eddies to and fro
By pier and alley, street and avenue:
   The myriads stir below,
   As hives of coral grow—
Vaulted above, like them, with a fresh sea of blue.

NEW YORK, JULY, 1863.

(In the University Tower.)

Is it the wind, the many-tongued, the weird
  That cries in sharp distress about the eaves?
Is it the wind whose gathering shout is heard
  With voice of peoples myriad like the leaves?
Is it the wind?   Fly to the casement, quick,
And when the roar comes thick
          Fling wide the sash,
          Await the crash!

Nothing.   Some various solitary cries,
  Some sauntering woman's short hard laugh,
Or honester, a dog's bark—these arise
  From lamplit street up to this free flagstaff.
Nothing remains of that low threatening sound;
The wind raves not the eaves around. . .
          Clasp casement to,
          You heard not true.

Hark there again! a roar that holds a shriek!
   But not without, no, from below it comes:
What pulses up from solid earth to wreak
   A vengeful word on towers and lofty domes?
What angry booming doth the trembling ear,
Glued to the stone wall, hear—
            So deep, no air
            Its weight can bear?

Grieve! 'Tis the voice of ignorance and vice,
   The rage of slaves who fancy they are free,
Men who would keep men slaves at any price,
   Too blind their own black manacles to see.
Grieve! 'Tis that grisly spectre with a torch,
Riot—that bloodies every porch,
            Hurls justice down
            And burns the town.

THE WITNESSES.

PAST midnight, thro' the city hushed and chill,
Undreamed-of lodgers in the human mill
Seen but as filmy whiteness 'gainst the skies
Up from the crannies of the pavement rise ;

Rise from the lairs where all day long a tread
Of passers-by is echoing overhead
Whispering more truthfully what goals they seek
Than if with tongues the various feet could speak.

Damp and concealed in crevice and in nook
These presences, thin as the leaf of book
And spread far out like flaky growth of caves
Or wild-fire fungus on the walls of graves

Are sensitive as chemics to the sun.
Through their fine nerves unlying tremors run,
Though blind and voiceless, still and seeming dead
They hear what never yet in words was said

Of joy and agony man's soul within,
Of bridal yearnings and of graybeard sin;
The lover's hatred of his love; the growth
In hapless minds of thoughts they fear and loathe;

Anger past words which comes one knows not why;
Satiety before the cup is nigh;
Vague rapture that of conscience is the prize
And bliss too keen for coarser speech than sighs.

That nimble step tells one who works for need;
Yon groping tread, a man whose vice is greed;
The gait that minces, overcharged with pride,
Is one; another, the vain-glorious stride.

The gambler's emptiness, the generous spirit
Of him who grants his neighbors all they merit;
Trembling of drunkards, the unstable mind
Of thieves still listening for a cry behind,

The anguish in the murderess of her child,
The shame, alas, of her whom love beguiled,
A thousand secrets, whether good or ill,
Into those ears below the pavement steal.

So, ever speechlessly, when midnight stamps
Her shadowy heel upon the colored lamps
And the town-shine is caught against the clouds
In bands of pallor like gigantic shrouds,

When o'er the lights that join lines down the street
Wheels of strange rosiness the eyesight cheat,
And in the gloom below the beetling eaves
A redness suddenly the darkness cleaves,

The spectres rise! Unholy is their skill.
They crowd the square, yet scarce a key-hole fill;
Dancing a ghoul-dance o'er the silent town
They sweep on those whom fitful slumbers drown.

A BETROTHAL.

BEAUTY needs gold.   But what is there beside
In this betrothal where all friends deride?

Surely for this the parents are to blame
   Since, fond or careless, they indulged their child
   Till she at thought of lacking aught grows wild
And in the race for riches knows not shame.

And who shall say that sordid hope of gains
   Inflamed not those who brought her into life
And at the breast the milk had secret stains
   Of pride and avarice, of ambitious strife?

For look at her.   This is no vulgar form
   For clasping of a booby.   Are those veins
Channels for no great waves of passionate storm
   When empire love o'er the rapt subject reigns?

4*

Ah dainty feet, and dainty hard white hands,
　　Hands sculptured fair to toy with curls and flowers,
Small feet to stroll beside one into lands
　　Where haste comes not, where envy never lowers...!

Ye generous gifts of beauty travestied,
　　Transcendent colors of young cheeks and hair
　　Disfigured by that sharp look seen where'er
The wrangling brokers vie in money-greed. . . .

Hard-outlined form and clean-cut empty face,
　　Your joy's a business ; all alert, ambitious,
　　You're good because there's no time to be vicious ;—
The world's coin current must be commonplace !

　　So there she sits, alas the too apt scholar—
　　Merely the profile on a golden dollar !

TO A DANCE MEASURE.

MAIDEN with farsearching gaze,
As you waltz, as you drift through the maze
  Why blush that you love the deep motion,
Why speak of the dance in dispraise?

Winds always dance with the cloud
Nor are sea currents ever too proud
  To whirl with the ships on the ocean
With a lightness to liquids allowed.

Earth never stops her advance
Nor about her own axis to dance,
  While circling each House of the Planets
Not a slip does she make or mischance.

Planets encircle the sun
But the sun and the stars every one
  Revolve on those pivotal granites
That were central when earth was begun.

These again subtly may plod
With their feet by the infinite shod,—
   Yet all be a speck ever drifting
Through the veins of ineffable God!

Maiden with hair like the night
And a hue of the north-polar light,
   Who knows with what gay worlds and shifting
Yonder vein on your temple is bright?

Skies if you infinite call
Then within is the infinite small;
   Here stand we between, while the ocean
Of ignorance covers us all.

Time exists not, nor of space,
Nor of greatness or smallness a trace;
   For nothing is sure here but motion—
And the love that looks forth from your face.

Dance and delight and adore,
For the present what queen can do more?
   Swing free on the tide of emotion—
'Tis a breath—and your barque is ashore!

SPRING IN THE CITY.

THE streets are thick with human life
　　And men move slowly, now that spring
Has cut apart with golden knife
　　The fetters binding bud and wing;
Pale folk their stifling garret shun
And walk like languid flies in the sun.

The chambers of the sick are filled
　　With cooler air.　They hear the sound
Of men and wagons, long time stilled,
　　Once more through lifted sash resound;
In sunny vines by dry churchwall
The amorous sparrows chirp and brawl.

And workalassies drop their shawls
　　To loiter homeward in the light;
While bending cobblers hate their awls
　　And ragged boys forbear to fight,

Grown girls the season holds in sway
And lads their longings cannot stay.

For some unwonted inner heat
   Bears down on their young bosoms so,
They must be out and try the sweet
   Dull laming languor to o'erthrow.
The old ones sigh and smile and sigh
To think of spring in years gone by.

The river looks to men less chill
   And tarry boatmen lay their ways;
With tow the gaping seams they fill
   And soon with oars the water graze;
Now dockrats plunge them in the tide
And icebound fleets to market glide.

And reeking stokers quit their coals
   To snatch the breath of moistened fields,
While turfmen lounge with talk of foals
   And what in horse the season yields;
A landlord gives a kind good day
Though tenants are too poor to pay.

The street-girl smoothes her lazy arms;
  Forgets her dream of turfy grave
In hope that spring will aid her charms;
  While drunkards think they will be brave,
Softly his lash the teamster wields
And gamblers envy John his fields.

And all are moved in various ways
  Save one alone who trips the street,
A woman full of devious grace,
  Of ready words and glances fleet;
Her light robes might the spring beguile;
She hides a pale face with her smile.

Yet she has wrung her husband's soul,
  Her children's happiness she slew;
Her lover's hope in life she stole,
  Nor even to herself was true.
Her heart, if cut, like gray puff-ball
Into a fine black dust would fall.

GOATS.

CRUEL and yellow of eye,
  Coarse-haired, shaggy of side,
With a humorous low philosophy
  Does a goat this world deride.

Greedy, wicked and mean
  He butts when his mate would share
And munches his stalks with a leering grin
  At his neighbor's famished air.

Sneering, lustful and cold,
  None's viler under the sun;
Yet he might be the sweetest lamb in the fold
  To judge from his skeleton.

FRIENDSHIP.

Aн, is it not a bitter time, ay, is it not a mournful
    day
When, meeting of a trusted friend, his old eyes turn
    away?

What have you done? Alas, who knows! In kins-
    men's eyes you have not proved
By gifts your friendship; kindliness has not been
    paid for as behooved.

Perhaps his wife too often speaks in praise your
    name; perhaps again
With too much dark suspect of thought her utter
    silence racks his brain.

Or else she has a tongue to hint that friendship has
    its limits here
And house and home and wife and child than just a
    friend should be more dear.

Perhaps—perhaps . . . You vainly stride through
    dark surmises without end
And at the last it merely comes to this: That you
    have lost a friend.

SOME PEOPLE HAVE LUCK.

SIDE by side upon the deck
   Lounging, she and I :
Little did the other reck
   What should hap thereby.
Strangers! Which perceived the other?
   'Twas nor she nor I ;
'Twas the evening's fostering mother
   Lamping in the sky.

Listless both the shimmering river
   Watched with dreaming eye,
Watched the spectral vessel shiver
   Gold that poured from high,
Throwing shades fantastic, black
   As across they fly,
Stamping on the yellow track
   Forms of sharpest dye.

Softly, soft our shoulders moved,
   ('Twas nor she nor I,)
And a languor strange behooved
   That (she wist not why)
Little weary head adrooping,
   Worn with lessons dry,
Now upon my shoulder stooping
   Fell with childish sigh.

Calmly in the moonlight sleeping
   She nor stirred; and I
Scarcely dared a breath while keeping
   Watch for waking sigh.
When it came and head flew back
   All that she could spy
Was a sleeping youth—a track
   Of gold—the bay, the sky!

She, an earnest artist-maid;
   Broker's clerk was I.
The shoulder where her cheek was laid
   Grew so bold and spry,

It has forced enough concession
   From the world a shy
Modest house, a wee possession
   With hard gold to buy.

Now, when night the bay is steeping
   In its sable dye,
Here's a little head asleeping
   That same shoulder nigh.
Busy brains now plan for me,
   Hands for poor me ply:
O saffron wake across the sea,
   Who's so rich as I?

HOUSEKEEPING.

DECK your house from inward out.
  Let there be an inmost shrine
Where to praise with gifts devout
  Love both human and divine.

After that, the holiest room
  Heap with choicest things that grow;
  Spare not gold or silver show,
Ambergris, nor forest bloom,

Man's wrought marvels daintiest,
  Colored canvas, chiseled stones,
Comforts few, but all that's best,
  Each that special beauty owns.

Then as worldly station calls
  All your home in order set,
  Nor through hasty pride forget
Chambers still outrank the halls.

After, if you more can spend,
   Neatly decorate the shell ;
Next your crumbling fences mend,
   Lay your road-beds deep and well—

But beware, lest these beguile
   Care on outward things to waste :
   Save in chambers fair and chaste,
Where does fortune really smile?

THE WEEK.

PUT Sunday aside for your prayers and your think-
    ing ;
  Monday for reading and writing and dreaming;
On Tuesday be battling, be sweating and swinking;
  On Wednesday be acting, be busy and scheming;
And feast ye on Thursday with eating and drinking.
On Friday be sure that you cuddle your wife ;
And sadly on Saturday muster your life.
Who the rules seven severely applies
He shall be good, healthy, wealthy and wise.

ON A FIREFLY SEEN IN TOWN.

WAND'RER through night,
That o'er the town urgest thy random flight,
    A lamp displaying,
    In vain assaying
To lure a single comrade towards its cheery light—
    Here be no friends at play;
    No bird of prey
Marking the gleam will swerve aside in fright.

    What brings thee here
Where all is dust and brick? where buildings rear
    Their summits dreary
    Like shoulders weary
Of basalt giants in a crater's frozen mere?
    Where the streets ooze with death
    And every breath
Is perilous from a feverish atmosphere?

Why onward speed?
Far lie the whispering meadows; in the reed
　　Sparkle thy joyous brothers
　　Till daylight smothers
Their dance, their garish tapers 'neath the danksome
　　weed—
　　Galley, whose sails ne'er droop,
　　From off whose poop
Signals are flashing which no comrades heed!

　　Or hast thou mind
To scorn their joys, and, spreading all unkind
　　Thy pinions slender,
　　Dost hope to render
Thyself more wise than they, and thine own eyes less
　　blind?
　　Haste thee, return, untried
　　Leave all beside
And thoughtless foot once more the evening wind!

　　Perhaps, a sage
Thou far'st abroad in fierce and cynic rage
　　Thy lantern blowing,
　　Too surely knowing

No honest man may live and walk this lying stage.
   Halt! the town bricks are hot
   And no green spot
Exists that can thy fiery heart assuage.

   For who shall say
Thou hast no errand? that no thoughtful way
   Thou here pursuest,
   And what thou doest
To-day is not well done as it was yesterday?
   Thou hast a heart so stout
   I fairly doubt
Thou dost the work to-night—and I the play.

   Where didst thou gain
That flambeau lighting up the aerial main?
   Was it in runnels
   Of earth, in tunnels
Deep underneath the ground that, tricksy miner, fain
   To suck volcano juice
   Thou could'st produce
Sulphury quintessence without smoke or stain?

Seen, then unseen—
Thou art a wizard with the night for screen;
    Or, from a pyre
    A drifting fire
That in the fitful blast grows ruddy red of sheen;
    Or, a mere bubble of gas
    Burning doth pass—
And darkness hath forgot that light hath been.

    Where woods are dank
Thou spiritual incandescence from a bank
    Of weeds miasmal,
    Thou gleam phantasmal
Art proof of hidden good that lurks in all things rank;
    Insect, or streak of fire,
    Thou dost aspire
To live on high a life not always blank.

    Perchance thy track
Is seen by Someone's eye.   Do light and black
    In varying sizes
    Reveal surprises

Of secret telegraphy?—not for us, alack!
　　Dost thou with night and fire
　　Write thy desire
One instant on the shadowy chimney-stack?

　　Nay, nay—no fly
But sparks thou art from wheels no man can spy.
　　The fays are stirring!
　　On crystals whirring
They meet, and when they clash, long flashes greet the
　　eye　.　.　.
　　Yet the light shines too smooth,
　　Thy gleamings soothe
Like slumbrous stars that dream within the sky.

　　Why then—of life
The Lord hath touched within yon home a wife,
　　And that quick flashing
　　Is but the dashing
His torch makes as he lights a human soul to strife.
　　May the flame clearly burn
　　Until its turn
Cometh to fall by death's druidic knife!

A taper, thou,
Held by that hand to which all mortals bow!
Thine innocent gleaming,
Is only seeming—
Thou com'st to summon silence to a tortured brow.
Resting some roof upon
The thread long spun
Is snapped, and life is over! who knows how?

Alas, this age
Lets nothing extant be on Nature's page
Save when through fences
Of our seven senses
They pass to where king reason struts his crumbly
stage.
Thou if not angel art
Perchance a part
Of fiery ethers round the pole that rage:

A little coal
From wintry conflagrations o'er the Pole—
From flaming mountains
Of snow—from fountains

Of fire essential, just one spark that downward stole!
    So, wand'ring from that sphere,
    Thou dost appear
Alive to those who languish toward a goal.

    Or from the sea
Wast thou in midmost of a storm cast free?
    Hath Luna's crescent
    Drawn phosphorescent
And life-like spray on high and lent it wings to flee?
    Art thou of amber made
    Or wave-tossed jade?
What is thy meaning, brilliant mystery?

    Ah, now I know.
Thou art the soul of one, whose heart was so
    Unmoved, disdainful
    That from the painful
Mishaps of man arose no ruth, no kindly glow.
    Here thou didst squander years
    And here thy tears—
If thou could'st weep—would testify thy woe.

It is too late:
To thine own choice of life thou'rt dedicate.
    Harsh was thy laughter
    And mock :—' Hereafter?
Who knows thereof? Drink deep, feed high, but
    cease to prate!'
    Now, a poor wind-blown fly
    That knows not why
Thou hast that earth which seemed the loftiest state.

    So, thou art come
Blindly revisiting thy human home ;
    Thy heart, once ashes,
    Now vainly flashes
With ghostly heat that warms not, though it stars the
    gloom ...
    Yet—God thee bless, sweet fly,
    It may be, I
Defame in thee the fair night's loveliest bloom.

OF A POET IN TOWN.

YOU ask me why, O lady gemmed and fine,
  The mystic singer proved beneath the gas
  No thrush of the woods, no lark that loves the
    grass,
But mocking man like all the dreary line.
You asked me why, and I have found, alas
  The reason true.   The poet is all strings
Of coarse and cobweb, where all winds that pass
  Ring out what notes they bear upon their wings
And count the noise the poet's.   But he knows
  They're vanishers by their own voice condemned,
And, wise in thrushes, likes your rustling gown.
  Wherefore it comes, O lady fine and gemmed,
He pulls what brilliant scentless flowers the town
  May nourish; you, what in the shy wood blows.
    5*

(For the Two Sides of a Fan.)

WHERE the jets of sunlight pour
   Through the damp shades on the brook
   Who is this that scarce has shook
Morning from her pinions four?
   Dewy joyous diamonds glitter
   On the blue wings of this flitter
In and out where violets sag.
   When the flickering body settles
See what flash of precious metals
     Sits and quits the swaying flag!

Hers are wings cut odd for pleasure,
   Curved for sporting, not for toil,
   'Twixt them in a dainty coil
Runs the purple gold-green treasure
   Fashioned for a life capricious,
   Blind to all things virtuous vicious

Only skipping what offends.
 She is called by men the Maiden
 Fashioned, more than flower she's swayed on,
For luxurious wanton ends.

Curtained in an alcove dim
 Half in white light, half in umber,
 Now in motion, now aslumber,
Purple-bodiced for a whim,
 Who is this with lines that beckon
 Looks whereon no man can reckon,
Frowns for lovers, leers for friends?
 She is called by men a maiden
 Fashioned like the couch she's laid on
For luxurious wanton ends.

SONG FROM "SINGLE-SCULLS."

WHY is the oarsman gay?
  No pleasures pall
On joyous hearts that stir the piny wings;
  Where seamews only play
  His shallop skims away,
Away o'er deep and shoal like leaves in fall;
  Blithely his red blood swings
Along his veins and burns them clear of gall.

Boatmen shall envy whom?
  Not the poor wight
Who checks a steed and follows his caprices—
  A pampered charger's groom
  Whose soul has not the room
To hold the oarsman's hot and ceaseless fight!
  His puny frame he pieces
With legs of brutes, and braves in alien might.

Boatmen demand no aids
    From sail or beast or steam,
But cut the wave in their brown strength rejoicing.
    Should bayonets grow from spades
    They'll change for swords their blades
And cut with might the ruddy battle-stream.
    Ho, for the oarsman poising
His brawny back under the live sunbeam!

IN CENTRAL PARK.

DID you know? when we gallop,
  My horse and his rider,
I see my lost love;
  I gallop beside her.
There she rides broken-hearted
That maiden departed
And farther away than the isles of the sea.

My dear is not buried,
  My girl is not drowned,
My laugh is unworried,
  With praise I am crowned;
She dwells in the city
Rich, wedded and pretty
Among her own kindred five minutes from me.
  I seldom espy her,
  Avoid her when nigh her,
She is farther away than the isles of the sea.

But, strange! in a gallop
   I turn broken-hearted
The wraith of her old self I meet.
   She's alive, though departed;
   Though honored, a robber;
   Though smiling, a sobber;
   Though trusted, a cheat.
For her body soft clothing;
   Her soul, hidden loathing;
Her mind—not a sentence complete.
   She canters so near me
   I feel she must hear me
Though I know 'tis a falsehood I see.
   But when at my talking
   My horse falls a-walking

Though I yearn, though I sigh to her,
   Speak to her, cry to her—
She is gone farther off than the isles of the sea.

MAY, 1874.

I PACED a mighty town from end to end,
   And who d'ye think I found was happy there?
   Of joyous sign street after street was bare
Until I came o'er a dry fount to bend
   Where two lean curs, racing in endless fun,
   Paid a glad homage to the insulted sun.

POEMS OF OTHER LANDS.

AN ARAB?

YES, like an Arab, sworn the desert still
  Shall hold him gaunt within its virgin bounds,
  Like him I march. For he perceiving sounds,
Sees through the gateways of an arid hill
Wide gleaming lakes where birds of luscious notes
Swing the green palms to throbbing of their throats,
Where flowers expand, whose face, eyes, ears form
    one
Clear trembling cup to drink of the filtered sun
And mark the time to harmonies begun.

Yes, like the Arab. For the fine reins fret
  His slender mare, and, whirling in his seat,
The rider stares. What hankerings beset
  His dry thin frame and stirrup-weary feet
For yon deep reeds, yon little waves that smile
About the grass roots! Was it worth the while
Such blisses in this brief life to forswear?

But, sworn being sworn, mayhap the prairies there
Are thin mirage and pictures of the air!

Yes, like the Arab.   For he may not bide
   Should these be real; but false—why, then he may
   Prick with his spear their shadowy array
And chase the enchantment o'er the desert wide.
But if... but if...!   The senses are not clear
When long the sun has charred, and hideous glare
Of baked gray plain to weary brain has stung,
When heat roars past the ears like anthems sung
Deep down in hills by many an Afreet's tongue.

Yes, like the Arab.   For to-day, who knows,
   Though all were true, his foe may not, the Turk,
   Within the bosquet by the water lurk,
A scourge God wields to pay for broken vows?
Far better, sands were o'er his body rolled,
Than steed and man were into bondage sold.
Thus, like the Arab, I too see what's fair
Soft and enticing—and as little dare
To prove the dangers that await me there.

THE BRIDE REPENTANT.

PALE was the bride. As in a tower two dusky lamps
    are set
Her eyes lit up her slender frame from zone to car-
    canet.

Upon the board a foamwhite cloth with isles of silver
    strewn
Lay stretched between her and that heart she once
    had called her own;

And as the heavy darkling wings of moths at night-
    fall flee
Toward deadly flames, his sombre thoughts forever
    crossed that sea.

Then who of all the guests could read how kissed and
    passed and came
Those looks of hers that seemed to freeze, those icicles
    of flame?

Who saw him slide among the flowers a little paper
    white,
Among the roses sent in sport across the board so
    bright?

Would she accept? For one long breath his fate in
    balance hung;
Then in her glove she slipped it quick. Warm lay the
    snake and stung.

The feeble churl she was to wed grew pallid at her
    mien;
She rose and sauntered toward the door—to greet
    them soon, they ween.

But o'er the hill where red's the moon two lovers wend
    their way;
With groan and tear for many a year that churl un-
    wed shall stay.

THE SISTERS OF FINISTERRE.

"For me he came; I drew him here
   With my brave locks of gold.
Then who are you to make him cheer
   You black-haired huzzy bold!

"Think not to own what once was mine,
   Await no ruth from me,
Who bade you round his heartstrings twine
   Your false simplicity?

"See you this bodkin? When alone
   In dreams of him you burn
From slumber soft without a groan
   A pale corpse you may turn!"

———

The younger wept and prayed and moaned;
   She barred her chamber door;
But at mid night, sans word or sound,
   Claire stood her bed before.

Young Renée from her tender paps
　　Has tossed the linen white.
The greedy moon her color laps
　　With its small tongues so bright.

On the left side the elder pried
　　Softly the wrapper off.
That sobbing heart could be descried
　　Still quivering from the scoff.

But soon, a ruby humming bird
　　Caught in a flower of snow,
It heaved no more.　Without a word
　　Claire struck the small sharp blow.

THE FOUR KONANS.

(*An Irish Legend.*)

WALES, A.D. 560.

MERRILY clanged the harps, and shrill the pipers
  blew;
Around the royal banquet jest and laughter flew;
When in by open doors a stranger, blithe to see,
Marched with a joyous air and bearing brave and free.

He stayed not with the lowly, nor stopped he at the
  salt;
Upon the king's own platform lightly did he vault;
He swept aside the steward, who asked him of his
  rank,
And 'twixt the royal pair upon the bench he sank.

No shield against the wall his place had told to him;
No question would he answer, that hero brown and
  slim;
Upon the jeweled cup a careless hand he stretched,
His dagger from the king's plate a haunch of venison
  fetched.

6

" Beware, O hero ! " whispered the steward in his ear,
" Yon champion of the black look, who reacheth for
    his spear,
Hath rights on every marrow-bone that comes upon
    this board :
Crack one with reckless hand, and crowns must crack,
    my lord."

The stranger laughed, and quaffed with lips as cran-
    berries red.
All golden were the curls about his shoulders shed ;
His eyes flashed blue as ice when north winds yarely
    blow ;
His forehead had the splendor of newly fallen snow.

He stripped of meat the marrow-bone, and grasped it
    by the heel :
" Here hast thou, doughty champion, thy rights upon
    this meal ! "
He cast the bone like lightning that champion in the
    face,
Who moved nor spear, nor uttered word, but swooned
    within his place.

Then up rose all the household, with javelin, targe
    and sword;
And up rose that tall stranger, and beat them from
    the board.
A rain, a hail of mighty blows he cast upon the crew;
But ever on the frightened queen sweet looks and
    mild he threw.

" Now hold ! " the Welsh king ordered; "let all once
    more be set,"—
Though with his massive weapons his aged fingers
    fret,—
" A champion great is here, and though concealed his
    name
Well knows he how to guard him from slight and
    blame and shame."

"O, wondrous youth," entreated the brave queen
    where she sate,
" Tell me thy father ! " "Comely queen, I spring
    from Adam great.
My mother was a queen, yet Eve was not her name;
She was as like thyself as sister-twins are same."

"Pledge me, O champion, pledge!" she cried, "I love
    thy sparkling face;
Alas, like thine was once to view my darling Konan's
    grace.
But what is that I see? How cam'st thou by the
    ring?"
"That?" said the youth. "It is some spoil my father
    home did bring."

Then rose the wan queen moaning from that un-
    toward repast
And in the flames her diadem, her royal wimple cast;
"It was my son, my Konan, thy cruel father slew!
Oh, who of all my household will wreak his death on
    you?"

The hero bounded after, and caught her by the arm:
"Mother!" he whispered; "silence! Thy Konan's
    met no harm.
Behold thy Konan safe, and, grown to man's estate,
By land and sea in battles become a hero great!"

The queen her wailing stinted. "Right soon will
    shine the truth!
Bare me thy shoulder quickly, thou fair and god-like
    youth!
Lo, here beneath the white skin I thrust a shred of
    gold;
O king, rejoice! Rejoice ye, men! Here stands my
    Konan bold!"

The great king roared with laughter, and turned not
    once his head:
"This day a year three champions that self-same
    fable said!
The first we called the Ruddy. His eyes were green
    as grass.
For one year's proof I bade him go and round all
    Britain pass.

"Next day came Konan Fair; my son he claimed to
    be:
Light were his locks; a hundred were of his company.

Scarce was he gone when Konan (but he had curls of
    brown)
With thrice one hundred sworders approached our
    royal town.

"Now Konan Red, the wealthy, and Konan Fair, of
    steeds,
And Konan Brown, the joyous, who boasteth mighty
    deeds,
Will back return to-morrow. But, ere the day is
    done,
All Britain shall be certain which Konan is my son.

"So Konan, thou the fourth, whose thatch with gold
    is set,
Wilt find thyself to-morrow by threefold Konans met.
Back to our feast! for thou a comely champion art;
I wish thee well. My son or not, fall to with joyous
    heart!"

—————

With a Druid's wide eyes young Konan the Tall
Leapt from his couch at the peep of day:
"The sky in the west is red! The fall
Of Konan the Ruddy I soothly say.

" Konan Fair !—
Blood's on the cloud in the east!   For thee
Hope there is none ; in thy maid-fine hair
Blood ere the evening shall be.

" Konan Brown !—
Light is the north, where thou comest in pride !
Safe is thy life, though fortune may frown ;
What guardeth, I wonder, thy side ? "

———

To the narrow deep river looked Konan the Tall ;
With clangor of arms strode down from the ridge.
The heroes were coming.   First, ruddiest of all,
One champion set foot on the bridge.

" Konan the Ruddy, whom fine satins clothe
Halt, and give answer !   What longest thou most
To see the bridge full of ? " " Of gold," red-hair quoth ;
" Of gold and of jewels a host."

" Ha ! " answered Konan the scoffer, " thou'rt red,
But Konan art not, nor a royal son !
The offspring of merchants or chapmen instead ;
See, thus in thy shamming undone ! "

Over the bridge flew Konan the Tall,
Beat up his guard and clove through his breast.
"You are right," cried his spearsmen, "well earned
  was his fall;
That a chapman he was, is confessed!"

O'er the hills to the stream came Konan the Fair
From eastward, brave with his warlike band.
"Now halt," cried the hero, "and answer bear.
What would you the bridge here contained?"

"What, bold asker? why cattle and steeds,
Oxen and sheep to the brim!" he replied;
"Aha!" quoth Konan, "then those are thy needs?
Fair liar, the grave be thy bride!"

Over the planks rushed Konan the Tall;
The sword-play was sharp, but he humbled his crest.
"'Tis plain thou wert born as a farmer!"   And all
Those followers replied: "Thou hast guessed!"

Last of the heroes came Konan the Brown
With stately companions from out of the north.
"What would I the bridge were set with? A crown
Of heroes! of foes of my worth!"

His brow all perplexed stood Konan the Tall
Propt on his sword.   " Thou art prince, indeed ;
Yet claim'st to be Konan ? "   " My claim it is small,"
Quoth the brown-locked one, " as I rede.

" I am not Konan.   A Norman king
My father is: he hath sons five pair ;
And so the round world on adventures I ring
Some childless monarch to heir."

Over the bridge stepped Konan the Tall,
Reached him, laughing, a brawny hand ;
" I am Konan," he spake, " but whatever befall,
We will sword-brothers be, on sea, on land."

6*

ULF IN IRELAND.

(A. D. 790.)

WHAT then, what if my lips do burn,
    Husband, husband ;
What though thou see'st my red lips burn,
Why look'st thou with a look so stern,
    Husband ?

It was the keen wind through the reed,
    Husband, husband :
'Twas wind made sharp with sword-edge reed
That made my tender lips to bleed,
    Husband.

And hath the wind a human tooth,
    Woman, woman ?
Can light wind mark like human tooth
A shameful scar of love uncouth,
    Woman ?

What horror lurks within your eyes,
        Husband, husband?
What lurking horror strains your eyes,
What black thoughts from your heart arise,
        Husband?

Who stood beside you at the gate,
        Woman, woman?
Who stood so near you by the gate
No moon your shapes could separate,
        Woman?

So God me save, 'twas I alone
        Husband, husband!
So Christ me save, 'twas I alone
Stood listening to the ocean moan,
        Husband!

Then hast thou four feet at the least,
        Woman, woman!
Thy Christ hath lent thee four at least,
Oh, viler than four-footed beast,
        Woman!

A heathen witch hath thee unmanned,
  Husband, husband!
A foul witchcraft, alas, unmanned:
Those saw'st some old tracks down the sand,
  Husband!

Yet were they tracks that went not far,
  Woman, woman;
Those ancient foot-marks went not far,
Or else you search the harbor bar,
  Woman.

It is not yours alone that bleed,
  Woman, woman;
Smooth lips not yours may also bleed,
Your wound has been avenged with speed,
  Woman!

What talk you so of bar and wound,
  Husband, husband?
What ghastly sign of sudden wound
And kinsman smitten to the ground,
  Husband?

I saw your blood upon his cheek,
　　　Woman, woman ;
The moon had marked his treacherous cheek,
I marked his heart beside the creek,
　　　Woman !

What, have you crushed the only flower,
　　　.　Husband, husband !
Among our weeds the only flower?
Henceforward get you from my bower,
　　　Husband !

I love you not ; I loved but him,
　　　　　Husband, husband ;
In all the world I loved but him ;
Not hell my love for Brenn shall dim,
　　　Husband !

He's caught her by her jet-black hair ;
　　　Sorrow, sorrow !
He's bent her head back by the hair
Till all her throbbing throat lies bare—
　　　Sorrow !

You knew me fiercer than the wolf,
  Woman, woman;
You knew I well am named the wolf;
I shall both you and him engulf,
  Woman.

Yet I to you was always kind,
  Woman, woman;
To serpents only fools are kind;
Yet still with love of you I'm blind,
  Woman.

I'll look no more upon your face,
  Woman, woman;
These eyes shall never read your face,
For you shall die in this small space,
  Woman!

He's laid his mouth below her chin,
  Horror!
That throat he kissed below the chin
No breath thereafter entered in:
  Horror, horror!

THE MAID OF THE BENI YEZID.

About 1840.

ZULEIKA! The Turk!! Zuleika, stand forth,
  If Arab you are to the core;
By the east, by the north
Euphrates down-pour'th,
  To the west is the marsh without shore.

Zuleika, be swift! Zuleika, our tents
  Are girt by deep marshes and foes;
To the south like a fence
A squadron immense
  Of Turks, while we slumbered, arose!

"Up, maid of the desert! If still the old stamp
  Lingers on in the seed of Yezid,
Deck your charms without lamp
And list for the tramp
  Of the mare never stranger has rid.

"You shall lead on our charge in the wild Arab
way,
  You shall rally the young men and old,
Like the hawk on the jay
We shall cleave through the fray:
  Your deed by the bards shall be told."

With pride, with delight, after old Arab wont
  For a bridal she decks her sweet form.
To the foe, to the front,
To the battle's quick brunt
  She is whirling the keen desert swarm.

When first on Euphrates the thousand-edged
  sword
  Of the sun the fog-serpent had gashed,
With one man's accord
The whole Arab horde
  On their foe like a thunderbolt crashed.

Then vain were the cannon of Omar the Turk,
  Sword or pistol-flash—onward they raced!
Short, sharp is the work,
In a dust column's murk
  Are vanished the sons of the waste.

But Zuleika? Alas, the mare is too frail
   That swerves from the cannon aside!
As birds on the gale
Are caught in the sail
   Entrapped is the desert's fair bride.

She has played, she has lost. With a firm pallid
     face
   By Omar the wrathful she stands:
" Dread lord, grant me grace
That here in this place
   Undefiled I may die by your hands!"

Then still is each pulse while Omar his brow
   Rubs clear of the wrinkles and cries:
" Not so, for I vow
That in Bagdad enow
   Of ladies shall welcome this prize!

" Fair bloom of the desert, a princess's train
   And honors henceforth you shall boast ;
When the year turns again
To the season of rain
   Choose your mate from the best of my host."

Zuleika says naught, but far o'er the plain
  Her heart follows after her kin,
From the eyes of disdain
Her tears ever rain
  As to Bagdad the horsemen ride in.

When the year turned again, was Zuleika a bride?
  With a Turk the proud maid would not mate.
Like a queen in her pride
To the desert they ride;
  All the city looks on from the gate.

Her tribesmen have come from the tents of the free
  For the maid they had mourned as a slave;
By each gay saddle tree
All Bagdad may see
  How Turks love to honor the brave.

" Farewell, noble Omar, and Bagdad, farewell!
  Your pleasures are not to our taste;
In the close town to dwell
For an Arab is hell—
  We must wed, live and die in the waste!"

THE GALLIC HERAKLES.

CLEAN-WITTED Lucian, world-wise traveler,
 Records one picture shown him by the Gauls
Which caused in that god-scoffer such a stir
 As when through scorn a childhood's legend palls.
 But wrath at seeing a Greek god bantered falls
When a hoar, grave-robed priest the reddening Lucian
  sees
And tells why Gauls appear to mock great Herakles.

There stands the god with features creased and swart;
 His back is bent and decked with lion skin;
His trembling hands a brazen club support,
 On lion's mane his hair streams white and thin.
 With smiling face he turns a brow serene
On a vast press of tribes, that, in a rabble rout
As worshipers and slaves still follow him about.

They beg to follow, and in sooth must needs,
  For round each suppliant's ear is wound a chain,
A hairfine chain of gold and amber beads
  Like links of sunshine on the morning main;
  And, as the sun will grasp in one the skein
Of jeweled beams converging, so do these ropes run
With stops of ambry gold to join that Smiling One.

Wonders yet more! The old man, laughing, juts
  His tongue between his lips, and lo, the tip
Is pierced, and lo, each several cord abuts
  Thereto and binds, nor can there one cord slip.
  Seeming to move, each slave would fain outstrip
His mate in haste and zeal; dearly they love their
    chains,
For each one feels that smile a guerdon for his pains.

The Druid spake: Your Strong God crushed the west
  And won, ye say, through prowess of his arm.
We say his strength was in his tongue compressed
  And that his words confounded those who harm.
  'Gainst eloquence we Druids have no charm.
His god-like, lightning force and weight as of a hill
Could have availed him naught. It was his gray-
    haired skill.

ON THE MYTHSTONE AT GRUTLI.

STAY where you are.   Have for your lot no scorn.
Ages ago yon bowlder-rock forlorn
Was from its mother-mountain fiercely torn
   On glacier's back from its primeval home
   Down the vast vales for centuries to roam.
To-day it is an altar where was sworn
The fall of tyrants.   Here was freedom born.

AMATORY.

HIST!

When bats encroach on swallows' ground
And cats no longer keep in bound,
When dogs withdraw and in the straw
The rats are rustling round :

When jealous shutters open wide
And humble folk at supper bide,
When lovers know of whistles low
And pretty knots are tied :

When sun has doffed his crown and gown
And, smoothing out his kingly frown,
Has laid to bed his weary head
Along his couch of down :

Then I have leave a song to weave
For one who would be whispered :
A night-blown flower . . . a listening bower. . .
And nothing save a lisp heard !

THE TALL WHEAT.

THE wheat-stalks bow on the mountain side
  (Here and there and around they go)
The wild winds over the acres ride
  And hammer the young ears low.
        A path winds through
        And thither come two
With souls like the tall wheat bending,
        They shun one another
        Lest sighs that they smother
Break forth—and their day have an ending.

The tall wheat over the pathway droops
  (Here and there and around it blows)
The wild wind laughs and a tress as she stoops
  Of her gold hair over him throws.
        One by one through the arch
        These timid souls march
Where the wheat makes a fine green awning.
        But why, past the hill,
        Are they sitting so still?
Hush—away! 'Tis their day that is dawning!

IN THE GREEN WOODS.

WHAT! you can see on every tree
  The little warblers billing?
And here canst be alone with me
  Not willing—willing?
From love abstain? O where's the gain
  Of precious moments' spilling?
Soon, soon with pain you'll sigh in vain:
  " I'm willing, willing! "

The glorious day, the balmy May,
  The buds of life you're chilling.
I'll hear no nay. In mercy say
  You're willing, willing.
The butterflies together rise,
  The thrush with love is thrilling;
Hide, hide your eyes! I hold the prize:
  You're willing, willing!

PRELUDE FOR THE HARP.

GIVE me music, give sweet glances!
 All I ask is in the phrase;
Melody the zest enhances
  Of the blaze
 Issuing from eyelids clear :—
Give me music, give sweet glances
 Sprung from hearts I hold most dear,
While the gusty sound entrances
  Ear and ear
 With the rush of angel bands. . .

Give me music, give sweet glances
 Till with close enwoven hands
One compounded soul advances
  Toward the lands
 Where is neither night or day. . .
Give me music, give sweet glances ;

They shall lift me far away
Far from envy's poisoned lances
From a clay
Wet by each malignant stream. . .

Give me music, give sweet glances,
Choose for me the loftier dream!
Let me weave celestial fancies
On the scheme
Set whereby the comet dances:
Music give me, lovely glances,
Give me music and sweet glances!

MADRIGAL.

BEAUTY'S not an empty mask,
Beauty's deeper than the skin,
  For within
Runs the blood of manly sires,
Thrills the nerve that lover-fires,
  Void of sin,
Fashioned with the purest flame
In some crystal-hearted dame:
  Sweet the task!

Lovely face is not a fool,
Gold hairs often deck a brain,
  Though the strain
Strong of wit is not her need,
So the world give ample heed
  To her reign!
Why should crispy-lippéd beauty
Go to wisdom for her duty,
  So she rule?

What is sweeter than the mouth
In the meeting of its fellow?
 Kisses mellow
Lurk in corners of the lip,
Else you ever downward slip
 By the billow
Of the dimple-dinted chin
Till the pulsing throat you win
 In the south.

Goblets amber-heaped are good,
Good are glasses slowly drained
 And unfeigned
Lives of generous love—by sorrow,
At the ill may come to-morrow
 Just restrained!
Fruit to eat and wine to sip
And to touch with rev'rent lip
 Maid and bud!

INVOCATION.

SCENT of the rose! . . .
Breath of the new-ploughed field and verdurous si
From copses budding! . . .
Myrrhs that the chafing boughs
Of aromatic pine-trees cause to fly
O'er coily fern-tops, studding
The layers damp of fronds that heap in long wi
    rifted rows . . .

Bloom of the quince
So firm and ruddy and tender to foretell
Crisp fruit and solid! . . .
Heart of the forest prince
Of odor nuttier than the sandal smell! . . .
And all ye marshes squalid
Whose fog a savory saltness pricks, whose veins
    clear tides rinse . . .

Hair of the night
Black where the stars glimmer in sparks of gold
Through tresses fragrant . . .
Breeze that in smooth cool flight
Trails a strange heat across the listening wold . . .
Breast of the coy and vagrant
Uncertain spring, beneath whose cold glows the great
      heart of light . . .

Clouds of the blue,
Crowned by the sun and torn by lightning-jag . . .
And joyous sparkles
In seas and drops of dew . . .
Ye smiles and frowns that alter where the crag
Glitters and darkles ! . . .
Hear me, ye blissful, that alone see why I call on you !
    7*

SONG.

THE man who is not faint with bliss
When he obtains his darling's kiss,
He knows not love; for him the snow
Is cold, and wet the way below;
The gale is harsh, and dark the night,
Like common mortals is his plight.

The warmth that quits her tender sides
A spicewind is that frost derides;
The crystal marvels 'neath her brow
Can melt gray icicles, I know;
But when she smiles, the sky grows clear,
The crocus springs, and May is here.

O kiss that passed in wind and sleet
What witchery sowed you 'twixt our feet!
From out the snow a ruby rose
Sprang glad : red petals swathed us close,
And couched us warm—sans hope, sans fears—
For ten long breaths, or ten short years!

SONG FOR WET WEATHER.

THE gloomier the day ,
And foggier the weather,
  The surer love will play
At breaking of his tether.
The murkier the weather,
  The nearer comes my may,
Fog-belts link together
  Those apart who stay.

Here's a kiss—away
Through the misty weather,
  Light as rides a fay
Straddling on a feather,
Fine as o'er the heather
  Skip the webs of May!
Love through wind and weather
  Always makes his way.

THE BLUSH.

IF fragrances were colors, I would liken
A blush that deepens in her thoughtful face
To that aroma which pervades the place
Where woodmen cedars to the heart have stricken ;
If tastes were hues, the blissful dye I'd trace
In upland strawberries, or wintergreen ;
If sound, why then, to shy and mellow bass
Of mountain thrushes, heard, yet seldom seen.

Or, say that hues are felt : then would it seem
Most like to cobwebs borne on southern gales
Against a spray of jasmine.   But the glow

Itself is found where sweet-briar petals gleam
Through tend'rest hoar-frost, or upon the snow
Of steadfast hills when shadows brim the vales.

BLUE IRIS.

AND have you watched the lily proudly stand,
  The blue pond-lily in the shallow reach
Where little waves incline her like a wand
  Ere lisping life out on the mossy beach?
Just so my love moves beautiful and slow
  To fine dance measures in her own wild fancies;
  All secrets fair are centred in her glances
And round her feet the waves of feeling flow.

But when she's by, so magic is their power,
  Of her gray eyes I see naught save the blue;
I may not ponder all her beauty's dower

  Nor feast mine eyes on a less heavenly hue;
Yet thirsty men will dream of cool stalks through
The exquisite azure of the iris flower.

SONG.

LIGHT, light, light is the hand of my love in the
    morning—
  Light as the foam, cool as the breeze, white as the
     day ;
Dear, dear, dear the vein that her arm is adorning,
  Blue as the hills, irises smothered in spray.

Warm, warm, warm is the shoulder I press in our
    roaming ;
  Kind as a pet, timid and brave, tender and true—
Hush, hush, hush, guess what I found in the gloaming
  Richer than roses, sweeter than wine, fresher than
    dew !

FINGERS.

WHO will tell me the secret, the cause
   For the life in her swift-flying hands?
How weaves she the shuttle with never a pause
   With keys of the octave for strands?
Have they eyes, those soft fingers of her,
   That they kiss in the darkness the keys
As in darkness the poets aver
   Lover's lips will find lips by degrees?

Ay, marvels they are in their shadowy dance,
   But who is the god that has given them soul?
Where learned they the spell other souls to entrance,
   Where the heart other hearts to control?

'Twas the noise of the wave at the prow,
   The musical lapse on the beaches,
'Twas the surf in the night when the land breezes
    blow,
   The song of the tide in the reaches.

She has drawn their sweet influence home
To a soul not yet clear but profound,
Where it blows like the Persian sea-foam
Into pearls—
Into pearls of melodious sound.

IN PRAISE OF LOVE.

WHEN true souls at last have broke
  Through the mist of petty ills,
Vivid as the sap in oak
  Love their every fibre fills.

Sweetness free from bitter lees!
  Life that knows not deathly stings,
  Sunburst that unstinted flings
New-born aureoles on the breeze!

Maddening kisses, kisses pure,
  Mixtures clear of heaven and earth,
Instant joys that aye endure,
  Solemn ecstasies of mirth!

Let one soul musician be ;
  One, the docile sounding chord :
  Which is, then, the loftier lord—
Gentlest finger or the key ?

Kisses tender, kisses chaste,
  And embracings void of heat,
Faults confessed and errors traced
  Make the tale of love complete.

Beauty seen in commonplace,
  Humbleness, self-sacrifice !
  True love can unlock the skies,
Find of God the certain trace.

Love has made a desert bloom,
  Piled the towers of a town,
  Won for thinkers high renown,
Plucked men from a miser's tomb.

Love has beat a mail-clad host,
  Stilled the politician's strife,
On a scoffer's lip the boast
  Turned to prayer for heavenly life.

Think you faith could have its birth
 Without perfect love of two?
What made Christ a god on earth?
 Love, that after death was true!

Kisses gentle, clean as soil,
 Sweet as wells to those who thirst!
 So another's weal be first,
Sorrow is of bliss the foil.

SERENADE.

WHEN on the pane your face you press
   The twin lights gazing toward the shore
   Are my two eyes forevermore.
Behold and weigh their dumb distress:
   Against that one sweet fleeting sight
   They bide them constant all the night.

The gray gull blown from out the sea
   That gains swift-wing'd your purple shore
   When far out grievous tempests roar
Is my embodied thought of thee.
   My world, so dry with hopeless drouth,
   Grows fresh at thought of one red mouth.

The wild-rose reaching forth a hand
   To grasp your robe on bridle path
   Be sacred from your gentle wrath,
It is my longing fills the land.

The grasses on each favored sod
Bow down to kiss where you have trod.

The winds that in the chimney blow
Are babbled words of tenderness
And tributes to your loveliness
The red leaves falling from the bough.
In love so wide and yet so rare
Each thing of nature asks a share.

FOR MANY LEAVES.

FOR many leaves about my high-perched home
I may not watch her fair-appointed manse ;
For many leaves I may not even glance
From mine on hill to hers beside the foam ;
For many leaves, however tempest boom,
I may not see that her dear roof is spared,
Nor even haste when the red bolt has flared,
To note the unshaken taper in her room.

But when the keen-edged sickles of the north
Shall reap my leaves, say, shall I not then look
From hill to shore athwart the blackened boughs?

Ah yes ; but all at a wide house forsook—
Chimneys from whence no kind smoke issueth forth
And unswept eaves piled high with eddying snows!

A SPELL.

SINCE you were mine what is't that lies
  Within my yearning palm?
Since mine you were, what is't that tries
  To stir my restful calm?

Since you were mine, I feel you still
  In hollow of my hand
Crunched fine and small as fairies will
  Beneath Titania's wand.

A winsome packet of delight,
  A kernel wee and fruity,
The pith of love and O the might
  And crystal fine of beauty!

Like fragrant inmost lotus-leaves,
  Or murmured words that bless,
Or dye that perfect truth achieves
  Through steel of faithfulness!

A monograph of sinuous lines,
　The humbird's iris throat ;
Or incense from cathedral pines—
　A songster's pearliest note !

Now mine you are, a spell of these
　Has nested in my palm
And, as the moonbeams stir the trees,
　It stirs me from my calm.

MAGNOLIA.

O HAVE you seen the tree that wears
On leafless limbs in yearning spring
A thousand white wax-candle flames?
Grim winter with his draggled wing
Not one of them to extinguish dares:
Their radiance all his bluster tames.

A mystic candelabrum 'tis
Silent, clear burning while we throb
With languor 'gainst some coming heat.
Myrrhs from a thousand censers rob
Of sleep our eyes; we feel the kiss
Of parted lips on brows and feet.

A stand of candles fit for kings,
For gods, for jeweled memories!
Yet was there One no eye hath seen,

A lamp so much more rare that these
Are earthly gleams and paltry things
To her, of pearls and emeralds, queen?

Betwixt the hours of twelve and one
A dreamer walking through the night
Beheld her bloom.   Ah, how he gazed!
The spring-god plucked her from his sight;
Now drain his red veins of the sun
Ere her clear vision be erased!

Ye are not less fair, blooms that stay,
With you be no comparison;
I love you, once her radiant maids.
Leant by your iron gate, alone,
My night of life is clear like day;
For moon, not glorious memory, fades.

A SONATA OF BEETHOVEN.

I. FREE.

IT sleeps.   The master's first soft prelude poured
A deep oblivion through its every vein.
It sleeps.   And slowly from the shape I drain
Myself, the soul within its tissue stored.
This instant one with it—the next I gain
Free air from what was my own self, and gaze
On limbs stung rigid with delicious pain
Plunged fathom deep within an opiate maze.

But I myself, the spirit, thus draw free
And widely float upon the sway of tide,
The swirl of tide and shadowy harmony
Too cloudy-great for that cold figure there !
But hark beyond !   Do I not hear beside
An undercurrent set I know not where ?

II. Away.

The moon is hid, but fractured moonstarbeam
Lies sifted fine on wood and hill and dale.
Within yon room how lieth still and pale
The house I kept!—and yet to smile would seem
As, now it bade me back, now forth to sail
Far, far away upon the shoreless air. . .
Is that a footstep on the outer stair—
Some friend who soon at those blind eyes will
　　quail . . ?

What then? I am fast fixed within a stream
Of hasting passion and must even float
Impatient and ecstatic ; for it grows
At last on me that my soul's centre knows
What shall be found ; as when from lover's throat
Come sounds to her that sleeping walks in dream.

III. Through Woods.

The moon is hid, but what mysterious shades
Gaze deep-eyed forth from yonder quivering woods !
The treetops 'wait a secret ; o'er them broods
A spell-bound hush, a shudder dim of glades

Ere fall the dread tornado's panther moods:—
Though the beast springs not, yet they lean anear
And, fain to shriek together in their fear,
Brace them against soft ruin-ripe preludes.

But can I keep from drawing toward that dark,
And can I aught but merge my dim outline
With thickets gray, black trunks of the forest stark,
With awed and moveless spaces 'neath the pine?
I'm borne one way, a peal an outlook horn
Blows clear and smooth from fog-walled barque for-
  lorn.

IV. THROUGH MARSHES.

Beyond the wood, beyond the listening hill
The deep sea meadows watch the glimmering moon.
Right soon with cool her magic force shall fill
Their creepy hair, and from the clouds right soon
Bursting, on tawny reaches, wavering creeks
Her strange cold disk the dewy drops shall spill;—
Past which my yearning sound-borne outline seeks
A goal half-known.   Is this the gaunt windmill

Those knew that were my feet, and, past the pears,
Is this the homestead that my former frame—
That body moveless at the step on stairs—
Frequented?   Lo, is yonder sash the same
That, lifting, raised me many a night to heaven,
That, ah, fast closed, to many a crime has driven?

V. HOME.

A wind has blown across the whispering marsh,
A gale has torn the smooth moon-veil to shreds,
On rusty hinge a shutter grindeth harsh
And ghostly footsteps halt along the leads.
See, the sash moves!   A pale and blue-vein'd hand,
A tender oval whiteness flowed about
By wind-puffed hair, wherein slow burning stand
Two diamonds set in opals, solve the doubt

Of who I am and where.   She knows me near;
She lays grief-weary lips against the gale.
What is't to me that she is pale, so pale,
When soon to me her soul shall issue out
And all is done?   What is it, though I hear
Miles back a frightened knock, quick steps, a piteous
        shout?

VI. NIRVANA.

The moon is out, the wind is up, and now—
Leagues, leagues away across wide-writhing grass
And tossing trees where I of late did pass
Forefated, straight as flies the unsated crow—
I feel how hands a-tremble prove my heart
And hear husht voices, quivering sobs enow.
In vain.   Again that face shall never flow
With human grief, nor that cold smile depart.

But see, a pure lotus from its dusky sheath,
A sister moon just broken from her cloud,
She issueth white from many a parted wreath
Of dusky hair, and now she calls aloud
Some name once mine. . .
                    A flame!   Her clear soul's essence slips
To steep for aye with mine, from her fast-whitening
    lips!

MISCELLANEOUS.

SMOKE.

Across our round unwinking sight,
   Our shallow, wide and thoughtless eyes
There flutters something soft and bright :
   We watch it, ceaseless dancing, rise,
And, happed about by swaddling-bands,
First ope for it our half-closed hands.

Before we beg for sun or moon,
   Or things sea-grown or blown by land,
We lie on mother's knee and croon
   With hope to clutch its shadowy hand :
We scarce can be restrained from creeping
To where from golden core it's leaping.

And though we fear the figures spun
   Grotesque along its upward track,
Yet childish eyes are never done
   With peering up the chimney-stack,

While clouds that eddy thick and dim
May turn to witch or wizard grim.

Within its pearly jets a youth
   May often see a waved white arm:
Its shifting scenes have taught the truth
   To maidens flushed with sweet alarm,
Their foolish hearts once set a-beating
By feathery faces sly and fleeting.

The fumes of that sharp Indian weed
   Which blew disease from warrior's limb,
In lonely men such comfort breed
   Their meat is second to their whim:
Yea, myriad beauties twisting steal
Through careless eyes, till hard men feel.

O quick habiliment of grace
   From fire in liberal beauty welling!
Most free of gift, yourself in space
   With godlike bounty still dispelling!
Smiling, you mock close-fisted men
Who delve to hoard and hoard again.

But, cheerily you beckon him
   Who sees you crown a cherished roof
When waste of brain and chafe of limb
   Are borne for darling one's behoof ;
You streak in pledge the morning pale,
Or skyward scrawl a harrowing tale.

Along the jagg'd horizon rim
   Grandly your ocean runes are written,
Of friends who far in safety steam,
   Of barques the red-jawed worm has smitten :
Gaunt men who thread the wilderness
At sight of you kneel down to bless.

About the high altar's pyramid
   The cloudy ramps where incense chars,
Upward and upward lighter, bid
   The soul on earth frequent the stars :
When voices whirl those perfumed rings
God's mighty angels stir their wings.

A matin and a vesper rite,
   You speak of household light and gloom :
An old man sadly marks your flight ;

While in the silent close-barred room
A pastille, smoldering gently, saith
With scented finger, This is Death.

Light vanisher 'twixt earth and heaven,
    And sign of cool rest after heat,
To you the keys of peace are given :
    You're first, you're last a man to greet !
You seek, once clear of earthly strife,
The hush beyond the flame of life.

ON FORTUNY'S PICTURE OF THE PIPING SHEPHERD.

GONE is Hellas, fane and idol,
Gone are those symmetric men,
   Wise to bridle
Luxury with simplest regimen;
Yes, her temples are the robber's den.

Outer Goths and inner Vandals
Hurled the dainty columns down.
   Art her sandals
Dusted of the vileness that the town
Boasted 'mid the symbols of renown.

But the ocean held its azure
As when triremes smote the foam,
   Nor could treasure
Asiatic, in the grasp of Rome,
That befoul, nor shameful deeds at home.

Horns of tender yeanlings budded,
Grasses sang and flow'rets blew ;
   Sunshine flooded
Cape and steep with glory ever true,
Ruined isles with beauty always new.

On a time there seized a shepherd
Thought that caught him like the spring
   Of a leopard,
Forcing him aside his cloak to fling,
Pipe a stave, and wondrous wild to sing—

Not of Athens, nor the splendor
Of the arts in olden time
   But of tender
Tasks of love and deeds of manly prime,
Modern life in many a homely rhyme—

Sing his joyous lot in breathing
Winds of ocean, air and earth,
   And of wreathing
Dance and hymnal to the sunbeam's birth,
Crowns of ivy to the god of mirth.

As the flocks about him hovered
One from Spain who loved the old and new
    Him discovered;
When again his pipe he blew,
He with joy the pretty shepherd drew.

Who was he so gleeful-hearted
Save Fortuny, man and child,
    Who departed
Art from out the air and sea beguiled?
Art once more on Magna Græcia smiled.

GOETHE TO THE GERMANS.

(A. D. 1810.)

PEACE, peace—no more! Your jargon dulls my wits.
  What can you do to better your degree?
Though France be crushed, you'll still be slaves to
    Fritz;
  If France be strong, through her you may be free.
But when with cries as senseless as the herd's
  You hound men on to fight against the sun,
  Why, 'tis most like, ere summer be quite done,
That frosts will fall—with death to singing birds!

Farewell. I go to plunge me in the past.
  I can not stop your rant of foolish names
Like German, Frenchman, Russian, that are cast
  As walls across the pathway of those flames
Called Science, Letters, Art, from farthest east!
  Your national-nonsense will you then oppose
  To the deep Orient's shaping heat, that glows
Responsive to the heart of nature's priest?

Good-bye, good luck! Rouse me when chang'd your
    theme.
  I like you well, I love our German name,
But wars despise, quite sure that one good scheme
    For some great drama is far loftier game
Than thousand plots of kings, race-projects grand,
  Than wiles of chiefs who make men bale their hay.
  When leaders laugh, the peoples always pay.
For me—the wide world is my Fatherland!

DIOGENES ON ALEXANDER.

O ROYAL dog, O princely fool
   Standing betwixt the sun and me!
     Because I pray you stand aside
The sycophants who spoil your rule,
   The tyrants that enslave the free
And you, great Aristotle's tool,
     Stand gaping there with tushes wide
Upon this marvel that you see—
     A man with all his wants supplied.

O royal dog, O princely ass,
   Betwixt me standing and the sun!
     Had Aristotle so much wit
He would have given to you a glass
   Wherein are knotty clews undone.
Perhaps it then had come to pass
     That you my meaning might have hit:—
Your shadow has so bulky grown
   All Greece has got an ague fit.

YOUNG MEN'S FANCIES.

(JOHN GEORGE'S.)

GIVE me a girl with features small soft round,
　　With gentle hair and little flower-like ears;
Though few the haughty beauties in her found
　　　　And quick the tears;

Yet give me her who is at all points sweet,
　　That so, when I in watches of the night
Waking, perchance a horrid loneness meet,
　　　　A childish fright;

When I shall feel that I am all alone,
　　The only mortal on a desert globe;
Or sinking through the void like meteorstone,
　　　　Or crushed like Job;

Then, leaned across the dark bed, I may kiss
　　My bonny wife; what lips at random touch
Will soft and tender be, no highstrung bliss
　　　　Fierce overmuch!

Then she will murmur like a child asleep,
   But, her to guard, I shall at once feel strong
And to her praise shall frame, while slumbers creep,
   A silent song.

(ADOLPHUS ALGERNON'S.)

No pretty chits for me! A woman grand!
   A daughter of Anak would I had to spouse!
A strong-thewed vigorous maiden with a hand
   As broad as long; a wife that fills my house
With absolute sway—except where I the master
Rule, and she yield for fear of worse disaster.

Fair she may be, but not with even traits
   That hide the natural bias of the mind.
A strong defect I want that still betrays
   Some fault I love, although in nowise blind.
I'll have no doll-face lisping, helpless, gentle!
Give me a hearty lass, no lady sentimental!

With such at home, I shall adventure far
   And know, return will find a solid roof;
Fierce be our fights, but they will leave no scar
   For, peace being made, we shall not stand aloof;
Around her mighty waist my strong arms flinging,
We'll frankly kiss, fresh love from anger wringing.

Our children shall be lads of oak, not pale
   White lily-livered chicks with morbid minds,
Shall run and swim, shall dance and ride and sail,
   Draw strength from earth and valor from the winds.
Our sons with brain and back shall prove their muscle,
Our hardy daughters with the world shall tussle.

SURRENDER.

THERE lies a bliss just in the lion's jaws
   Ere yet his fangs crush to the very bone,
The while his dread broad soft unswerving paws
   Rest on a victim without cry or moan,
But keenly wakeful to his great warm mouth,
His yellow eyes, lovely, yet void of routh,
The cloudy mane his awful shoulders wreathing,
      His deep low breathing.

And there's a hatred for the being, too,
   That drags a wounded life among his kin ;
An instinct vile the helpless to undo
   And lick the creature dust of those that win.
As though 'twere needful to be baser yet
A longing sometimes will the bosom fret,
While garlands fresh the haughtiest heads are
    crowning
      To drown the drowning.

There's a strange luxury in being undone
  Crushed flat, brayed fine, wiped out and all de-
      stroyed,
A mighty joy to meet that glorious one
  Whose power is boundless as the unsounded void,
To feel a force that plays with you a while,
Takes your best life's blood for his lawful spoil
Till, fed superb by you, the careless render
      Stalks on in splendor.

Have you not felt it, that wild thrill of joy—
  Such joy perchance as the sad Hindoo feels
When priests drag forth their grim and giant toy
  And o'er his neck crunch the slow turning wheels?
Women, ye know what the sweet anguish is
In being o'erthrown, what though the giver of bliss
Be god or lion, ah, or manlike demon—
      Speak, O ye women!

9

TRUTH.

STAR of the wise,
Whose purple splits the evening blue,
  Whom meteor flash, nor stare of moon,
Nor touch of comet may subdue,
  Last night I read your rune:
    No gold or blue of Paradise,
Not dazzling heaven itself can screen
Ithuriel's diamond javelin.

OLD friends, books, chairs, old wine, old shoes
  Are things antipodal to shoddy;
They're sweet to love and playfully abuse,
  To laugh or cry with, rollick with or study;
Cherish them well, and you'll be sure to lose
  All bunions from your mental body.

————

  LOOK out and watch the river,
    Look up when stars are kind,
  Look round about you, whether
    'Tis rain, or mist, or wind;
  But never, never, never
    Look behind!

THE COMMONPLACE.

WHERE, O where's the commonplace
  Whiners tell me still they fly?
  Wheresoever falls mine eye
True things have their several grace.
Split the heart of commonplace
  And there's the Proteus—wriggling lie!

BOOZY LITTLE BAT.

BAT, little bat,
Up the chimney there what are you at?
Now that the Christmas clouds in the sky
Rattle with snowflakes, warm and dry,
   Wrapped in your soft leather wings,
Are you hooked up there by the toes,
     Do you doze
   Like Tommy the cat who sings
By the fender a bass to the kettle?
See him hang his head over the settle
   All upside down,
    You would think him done brown—
Yet he's in the finest of fettle!

     Bat, little bat,
Wherever you are you've a brick in your hat,
   Don't deny it!

How else, winters through
Cold you hang in a flue
  So quiet, so quiet
Head downward ?   Just answer me that, little bat!

Oh, the secret was told me :—
  A gnarl pated goblin (no matter
  What name! small bats mustn't chatter)
  Has blabbed, little bat,
  Of the brick in your hat
Every autumn—hush, hush now, don't scold me!
For he said, On the green
Where Titania the queen
  Of fairy-land held harvest revel
You were seen
  After dawn
  When the fairies were gone
Fie! drinking the dregs of the nectar potheen!

Oh, oh, who'd have thought
  You, batlet, a sot
Who dwell on so lofty a level!
Tehee, little bat,
So we find it is that

Makes you snooze without care ,
With your heels in the air
Though the draught be tremendous and ever so
hot !

But it's never too late,
Next year when you mate
And your children are fledge,
Come down to our fire
Small brown-coated friar
And sign, like a good Father Matthew,
The temperance pledge.

THE SEA SPRITE.

Nude as Adam rose from earth,
Bare as when you wept at birth,
Where the sand is wet and red
Near the edge of leagues of reeds,
Slumberous pools and trackless meads—
When with hands you've scooped a bed,
East and seaward lay your head.

Hidden there all breathless lie
While the sunbeams quit the sky,
Whilst above the cloudy west
Lingers still a virgin moon
Like the plume within the crest
Of a god who passeth soon.

If there be no mortal by,
Nor the mighty hush be broken
Save by gentle ring-neck's cry
Wailing with a grief unspoken,

Or by heron, booming harsh
From the vast and landward marsh.

If you fix a steadfast face
On the zenith's awful space
And your forehead seaward strain
Till the eyeballs rolling back
Trace the red sun's former track,
Till they catch at last the main
And the place whence daylight sprung—
Then look sharply through the gloaming
Past the broken swell and foaming,
Sharp the coming waves among.

Where the highest in its pride
Stalks with monster majesty
Is it magic that you see?
On the green and glassy curve
Whom do deadly breakers serve
As elephants for sport to ride?

'Tis the sea sprite. You have found
Where he tumbles at his play,
And with eyes below the ground
Ere the falling of the spray

9*

You can peer the wave-tops under,
You can view the ocean's wonder
Ere he dips and slips away :—
Careless madcap, seabeach-shaker
Quick to back another breaker,
Thus he sports till break of day.

Yet beware, one word but cry—
There's your grave dug where you lie!

LITTLE PEOPLE.

I STOLE so gently on their dance,
　Their pygmy dance in red sunrise,
I caught the warm and tender glance
　Each gallant gave his dear one's eyes.

Wee ladies clad in fine bat's-wing
　With pluméd lordlings stamp the heel;
Behind them swords and fans they fling
　And foot it blithely down the reel.

They sighed and ogled, whispered, kissed
　In meetings of the swaying dance—
Then fled not, but were swiftly missed,
　Like love from out a well-known glance.

I sprang: the flashing swords were grown
　Mere blossom-stalks from tulips tossed;
The fans that sparkled on the stone
　Were turned to sprays of glittering frost.

FAIRY LOGIC.

NEAR a stone
Thickly strewn
Nestle mushrooms cool and lowly.
Ask the dew
How they grew
While the owl was mousing slowly.
Frank they gaze
Through the haze
Their rooflets rearing o'er the lea,
Small but wise
By gay sunrise
Off the high land, down the sea.

People say
Fairies play
O'er these breezy uplands nightly.
Is it fable
That each table
Marks the place of banquet sprightly?

Come! would you
Prove it true,
Up, and ere the dawn be roaming;
Them in haste
Break and taste
Soon as fairies quit the gloaming.

You can tell
By their smell
And their nutty smack of good land,
You will guess
The essences
Found in marshes, moor or woodland;
You will know
Hills are so
Round and fresh and full of savor;
You shall say,
" Be what may
Only fairies lent this flavor!"

WEEPING WILLOWS.

I HATE a willow,—see it stand
Half in water, half on land
And its leaves the river sweeping
Tell of women ever weeping.
In the lowest of the valley
Where with fog the air is thickest
Evil spirits thither rally,
Poisons there infect the quickest,
And the tree that veils their nimble
Goblin-dances bears a symbol
In each earthward drooping limb
Yearning toward the waters dim.

Let no willow quickly grow!
If nor man, nor thunder-lighting
Shall be ready for its blighting,
Prune it close and guide it slow.
Better feed your kine with thistles
Than allow your children whistles

From the accursed wood to shape.
Through the hollow bark escape
Subtle humors miasmatic
That within the youthful brain
May engender thoughts erratic,
Longings, helplessness and pain.

But if you must ask the reason
Why the willow broodeth treason,
Why the vampire dim may skulk
In and out its spongy bulk—

You have forgot, I know, how the poor suicide
Snatched at its brittle boughs, and cursed it e'er he
died.

SELF MEASUREMENT.

No grimace,
Take your place,
Into the ranks with you !
Little brains
Bear no strains,
Play nasty pranks with you.
Just resolve
To dissolve
Your one crumb of salt,
Slowly rub
In the tub
Your one spoon of malt.
Bow your head,
You are weighed
No weightier than the next
No grimace !
Take your place
Who cares, though you be vexed ?

LIFE'S EPILOGUE.

O WRAP me in such yellow webs of silk
As swathe few months the painted midnight fly
And smiling lay me in the clean cool ground,
      Nor let the sound
Of screw or hammer vex me when I die.

Press the sweet soil upon my weary lids
And cool my lips with slowly trickling drops
And, if so be, let great roots lap my frame
      And pour my fame
Through harps Eolean of the wind-swung tops.

For thus I lie upon the grassy slope
And thus I crush my mouth into the mold
And this I mean : when I have reached the bourn
      Glad will I turn
To this dear earth which my two arms enfold.

Then shape no lead 'gainst natural corruption
But lay me so, for Indians of the plain
Raise high their chiefs no more; nor may I view
        From dead-cave of Peru,
Shriveled, the sun set o'er the vasty main.

There are who flit from here without a pang.
Men lived, who drained all wholesome joys of earth
And yet went hence without a groan or tear,
        No mournful bier
Made sad true hearts not yet beyond all mirth.

We live too much within our neighbor's brains;
Throng, but to fight; we drop good, hunt for crimes
Because our fellows seem to bid us—Fool!
        Why play the tool
To that ordain'd as you say by the times?

Men reck not you. Their own strings goad them on.
Choose your fit work and labor while you may,
So later years may haply bear a fruit
        From a strong root
And buy a grateful fame ere you have passed
    away.

INDIAN CLOVE.

THE VISION OF INDIAN CLOVE.

STILL, it smiled, this lonely land
Full of valleys set about
Low with crags that frowned in play
    When the spray
From a raincloud their dark faces tanned ;
Here dwelt joy without a doubt,
    Rest and peace ;
'Twas the spot from march to cease,
Pitch a camp and stretch the worn feet out.
Here had never farmer's fence
Scored the bottoms ; nothing save
Some chance birch bark, years gone by,
    Raised a wave
On the lakes that southward lie.
For the keen cut settler-sense
Took the left stream, took the right,
Filled the main vales with the might
Of the township, of the city dense—
All unwitting gave this range go by.

It was strange
Such a silence reigned throughout
All the region ! On each woodcliff range,
On the meadows, all the swamps about
Sang no bird, nor whistled any lark ;
Nor was heard the bark
Petulant of squirrels, nor the sad
Wail of hawk afar off; jeweled wings
Flashed no day-fly, nor in giddy rings
Whirled the insects that in ponds are glad.

So I thought: Meseems they hold their breath
Reverently, and watch far down the west
How, his agony in clouds confessed,
Lord of day is sadly done to death.
'Tis some magic, so they dumbly feel,
Foul and hidden, and to holes they steal
Fearful lest their god, this evening slain,
Come no more again.
So the evening wore into the night ;
But no bright
Flies of fire o'er their rushy bed
Lit the lowlands ; neither overhead
Star did flare, nor shoot a passing gleam,
Nor boom'd once a bittern from the stream.

Yet full soon are wrapped in leaden sleep
Way-worn pilgrims who have traveled far,
Though gray fear about their foreheads creep,
Though their heartbeats hands of coldness mar.
So the weights, that ever finely small
Added are each other to, were laid
On mine eyelids till a hueless pall
Hid the earth in one impartial shade.

Then within the middle night
    I sat upright.
Did one call? Did some wild beast
Break the silence that was domed
Bell-like over all from west to east—
That was tense, like metal, till the least
Cry re-echoed as the creature roamed?
No, some Thing that saw sans eyes
    Bade me rise;
That was tongueless, touching without hand,
    Gave command
Through enthralment of my will:
I arose, and set my face right tow'rd the hill.

It was steep—where splinters from the cliff
Clogg'd the long base with treacherous moving
    stone.
It was sheer—where the gnarl'd pine alone
Grappled for life with a grip past belief.
But o'er the waste and up the laddering fir
Tireless I climb'd to that hill's granite edge
And reached thin grass, and passed a thorny
    hedge
Into a wood.
        Oh then there came a stir
That stirred my hair at root! The leaves were
    light
On every tree, because a small foul worm
Had eat of each leaf half; a shivering fright
Rose from the limbs that never ceased to squirm;
But underneath, upon the empested ground
        No plant was found,
No summer bloom, no green sprout of a tree,
Nor aught but that great livid growth
Of rankest shade which all things loathe
Except the blowfly; he can never flee
Its fetid breath but, being lured, must die;

That, and the fungus on the trunk
    Which deep had drunk
Of deadly gas, of juices, till its dry
Tough veins were flaccid, soft and fresh
    Like brittle flesh ;—
These, and the Deadman's Pipe
    Which there stood ripe
Were all that lived beneath that creeping sound.

But I spake brave : However murk the ground
Or dank or foul, the wilderness is clean
Where'er of man no heinous deed has been !
And so press'd onward, quaking, thro' the wood ;
    Then, sudden, stood
At sight of four wheels rotting on the soil
While, grimly sketched in fantasm outline dim,
Ghastly, a mere poor flatness with a rim,
Lay beasts of burden fallen at their toil !

With that, what horrors seize
    My trembling knees !
    What nameless dread
Twists the wide eyeballs starting from the head
While through the wood towers a shape of fear !
10

What is it grows?   What is it fills the brim
Of yon deep pool from whose black borders sheer
Rise the light trunks?   What gleams through
    every limb,
Through ragged tops of deeply plunging trees
Off there, down there? No fitful, eddying breeze
Could bellows up and out those heavy coils
Of yeasty cloud in such unholy calm!
Yet now the wide Clove like a cauldron boils,
Now bloweth hugely smooth, as when a charm
Bids giant mushroom grow; and next it lilts
In steady circle round the valley's rim
While patterns vaguely woven out of steam
Indent the tent-like marvel as it tilts.
Nor do these rest; but evermore they swirl
In milky spirals, now like serpents curl
In, out, around, till each slow-modeling form
About, about, wheels in a still, wide storm.

Like him, who, standing on a whirlwind's brink
    Can only think
Of flight or hiding; yet like him, alas,
Who stares upon a jaguar in the grass
And see'th death, but can not break the spell
    Nor rightly tell

Why every limb is lame ; so on that night
Of awful journey I might never 'scape
The threatening storm but always I must gape
And, numb with fear, wait for the farther sight.

Then slower sped that vast revolving cloud
And, clearer cut, ran into solid groups
The nebulous pictures, till a panic crowd
Of children, boys, of women in wild troops,
Rushed madly hither, thither.   Nearer lay
Strong men in death, their foreheads lately gashed
By hatchet hurtled, or their bosoms flashed
Quite through by whining lead.   All pale were
    they
With features dumbly writhen.   Gestures wild
Were there of frantic women : some would save
Beneath full breasts a new-born tender child
And some with arms a boy ; some did but rave
And curse the foe.
                But that foe whirled around
The fenceless prey as dun wolves gaunt and
    grim
Will bait a buffalo : in every limb
Stick fast their fangs till on the slippery ground

He sinks unnerved; then echoes all the land
To senseless howlings of the hideous band.

Or was it sound, or did the harass'd sense
Of sight invent the far-off groan and cry,
The horrid whoop, the crash when some brain's
    fence
Was beaten down, each moaning, shout or sigh
That slowly rose and shook a distant knell
Down, down the years like some fog-muffled bell?
        Too real, too true
Came the sad clamor of the hapless few!

The fight was won, the pallid were o'erthrown,
The dusky swarm, as numberless as leaves
In middle year, were now all frantic grown
With victory. As reapers gather sheaves
So rioted among fair-braided slaves
The swarthy arms of particolored braves.
Then hardy muscles sharpened keen to lust
Throbb'd fiercely round some little piteous maid
Whose tender arms, rebelling, from her thrust
The foe's vile nakedness, but next, afraid,

She'd hide her face and droop upon the ground.
But of the slaves some few strong souls were
    found
Who, heart-strung by despair, while off their
    guard
The savage warriors turn from death to love,
Caught each a weapon and struck one blow, hard
And slew one man, and thus were glad enough
To sell their lives and earn the last reward.

But I, who with them died
    A thousand deaths
And with wild virgins groan'd and sigh'd,
Moaning at each new massacre of breaths,
    I stood all stone,
All helpless to assist them save by prayer,
By curse rebounding on the stagnant air,
    By wild threat thrown
Like his who raves within his own
Sad land of madness, where the spectres gibe
Forever at the maniac's diatribe!
Yet when the ebb, the folly of despair
Had cast me headlong on the rotting leaves
To hide the eyes from what no heart could bear,
Yet could I not refrain. There come reprieves

To bitterest anguish.   Was it wise and brave
To turn the face from horrors, first to rave
And then to fly?   I hastened to my feet.

What now was here, what changes fleet
Had swept the scene—pursuers, the pursued?
Do wolves turned lambs the victims thus entreat,
Do gentle souls refuse a mercy sued?
The forms are like, but every thin-flanked brave
Is full in flight or cowering like a girl
While on his track, or o'er him swiftly whirl
Pale shapes of fright like ghouls that haunt the grave.
Oh, blooming arms I saw that ruffians tore
From tender breasts aside! and writhen necks
Abhorring him who touched! ah, piteous sex
That suffered shame, ye are the prey no more!
          No, horrible with stare
From wide white eyes and mouths in cruel square.
          With bloody dabbled cheeks
Those victim-wraiths with heart-benumbing shrieks
Upon the spoilers leap.   No stoic mood,
No savage pride could brook that horrid scene,
But horror-struck the victors fain would screen
Their haggard eyes from the remorseless brood,

Would gladly hide
Like boys their warlike crests, would creep to holes,
Or plunge in lakes, or follow fast a guide
Who knew the trail to save their abject souls.

But there is none.   The cruel woman-hand
Is at their necks ; upon each shaven head,
On flesh of bronze they feel those tresses shed
Drops of deep-riving flame ; like acids brand
The cold blue lips, and when an arm is laid
About a man by ghastly simpering maid
He writhes, a panther that a serpent grasps,—
He screams, a child that a dim vampire clasps !

Yet how in words to tell
The foolish pity that thereon befell
At sight of firm souls crumpled like dry leaves
Beneath a fear ? at view of frenzied eyes
That awful terror of their pride bereft ?
To mark how, every moment, worse than dies
The grizzled chief who for his pastime cleft
The skulls of boys, and note the coward wail
Of braves once scornful of the leaden hail !

Why should it irk, why should it seem
Aught else but sweet that sufferers now redeem
With torture just the crimes and monster wrong
That they have borne? for unto them belong
Delicious vengeances, since now the stream
Has set their way. And so in one mad ring
The warriors fly; but lift in vain high knees
While at their shoulders livid women wing
A noiseless way and palsy-handed seize
On high warcrest or with keen filéd teeth
Touch the bare necks of foes until they shriek with
  fear;
But not one face that followeth hath a tear
Nor other thing each cruel eyeball see'th
Save that poor wretch alone who quaketh so
In flight before it round the circle slow.

  Yet now behold them haste!
   Faster the whole mass moves,
  Quicker, more quick, upon the pathway traced
Within the circuit of three hanging hills!
Now scarcely full the whole deep Clove it fills
   And soon in former grooves
Rides the wide dome of cloud, while all entwined

Are shapes of flight and following. Swift, more
   swift
On bellying tent the twisted figures shift
To spiral waves on milky whiteness lined.
A red light grows athwart the mighty sphere
       That itself ever drinks
       And slowly shrinks
With lessening borders, drifting from the grove.
But now the whirl is shot with rose from dun,
Now lit with sharp hues such as greet the sun
From Arctic ice-hills when the long night is done;
And now, compacted to a color clear,
       Calm, broad and near,
Only the moon, blood-red, stands over Indian Clove.

   10*

THE SEER.

THE SEER.

HISTORY is never written.   At the best
A fragmentary truth is half confessed
And quick denial follows.   Who in books
Of serious learning for real wisdom looks
Hunts clouds in rivers and as well may seize
The sunshine as it gallops o'er the leas.

In eighteen hundred ten an Indian seer
Still dwelt upon Manhattan.   It was here
He lived and died in fame most savory
Of virtue, healing power and sorcery.
And here he sang to trusty friends whose skin
Showed white albeit the heart was red within
The lays of old Manhattan.   Handed down
From sire to son of magical renown—
Whose cunning words and actions stranger still
Around the crowded wigwam sent a thrill,

Fired every heart and set the moccasin stamping
In furtive memory of the warpath's tramping,—
These songs at last, for shame of boors who scoffed
Crept out of sight within the mental loft,
Mind's garret of a white man.
Rescued thence
And gently altered to a clearer sense,
Behold the runes of ancient Greenland's fall,
The red man's flight, dispersion; last of all
The words prophetic uttered by that seer
Against the blatant race which lords it here.

Old was the chief, no Indian knew how old
And yet he stood erect, as calm and bold
As men of thirty.   Often by the hill
That scanned Manhattan then and scans it still
Beyond the brackish tideways, on the bank
Of lakelike Hudson he his camp-stones sank.
It there befell that friends by nights of wind
And cloudy wrack were wont to bend his mind
On days of old, and stir his wit with fears
Of goblins, or the woodhag who appears
All flame inside her skull.

On such a night
While huddling round the fire in panic fright,
When even the dogs in sympathy would moan,
Thus he his chant barbaric would intone:

THE RAID ON GREENLAND.

Mad wind! mad wind off the sea!
Tons of clouds before it flee.

Gray wolves! gray wolves overhead!
Hudson writhes within her bed.

Black, black the Palisades!
Fir-trees bow like willow blades.

See the cloud-forms northward flying,
Hurrying by without replying!

All the Indian clans are there:
Elk and beaver, turtle, bear,

Wolf and panther, moose and snakes,
North and west they whirl, as flakes

Foam along a mountain steep
When the spring-floods downward sweep.

Terror pricks them, and despair
Hounds them through the murky air;

Front they have not heart to show
When the dreadful east winds blow.

Listen, paleface, you shall learn
Why the Indians feebly turn

On the white man. 'Tis in vain
War shall burn and burn again:

Hear our nation's annals old,
What the seers, my fathers, told!

———

Six lives of a crow have passed
(Thrice will crows a man outlast).

Since in old and glorious days
Red men swept the eastern bays.

Indian warriors! hearts of bison!
Deft with arrows shod with poison;

Spears of copper, axe of flint,
Shield that laughs at hatchet's dint!

Tree-canoes of giant girth,
Camp-fires holding, stones, and earth—

Skins for sails and paddles great
Forest fashioned for their state—

Bore our chieftains far and wide
Lifting o'er the ocean's tide.

Far to eastward they had seen
Towns of white men, regions green;

Ha, they joyed not, till their hands
Ravaged all those sunrise lands!

Sungod's offspring was our leader,
Chief of all, our father, feeder.

Eyes of eagle, never bleared!
King-canoe ahead he steered.

North star led him.   On we sailed,
Eastward till our courage failed.

Icehills froze us; mermen splashed;
Sword-fish on our counters dashed;

Child of sungod never spoke:
Held us to our galling yoke,

Till we heard on Greenland's shore
Through the fog the breakers roar.

Night-time, night-time is the season
Pale men drink away their reason.

Night was round us.   O'er the town
Like red clouds we hovered down,

Hacking, stabbing, shooting, felling
Squaw, pappoose within their dwelling.

Burnt the stone-huts; those we found
Living in the embers bound;

Danced the wardance and with spoil
Homeward bent us to our toil.

Coast of Greenland, full of smoke,
Empty, black, forlorn awoke:

Towns in ruins, bodies gashed,
Children into pieces dashed,

Seacraft scuttled, cattle dead,
Naught alive our spears had fled;

Songs we shouted day by day
Till we made Manhattan Bay.

THE FATE OF THE INDIAN.

Wise the future to forgather
Magic knew my early father.

Cried he on the sungod's child
Who the nation had beguiled:

Sunchief, sunchief, you have broke
Faith and braved the white man's yoke;

As wood-devils clutch the backs
Of the deer within their tracks

For the crime of you and these
Curses on your race shall seize!

White men from the rising sun,
White ships o'er the sea shall run,

Thunder holding, lightning spitting,
Oaken shields as eggshells splitting,

Bringing poisons, fearful beasts,
Wasting all our corn in feasts!

Wizards are the blue-eyed race;
Them the airgod holds in grace;

Lends them wings; the thunderstone
Trusteth in their hands alone.

Once the air-snake gulped the sun.
So to death shall ye be done

Sunchiefs, by those men who are
Favored of the stormy star!

Manitou has sung me all,—
Theirs the victory, ours the fall!

Angry waxed the sunchild then,
Full of terrors vague, his men.

Prophet, prophet, stay your curses!
Cowardice your magic nurses.

Greater is the sungod far
Than the might of any star.

Clouds may hide his glorious face,
Yet they fade in little space.

Heavenly dragons that devour him
Only seem to overpower him.

Let the wrathful wizards come,
Never shall they see their home.

Cowards are they, babies, women!
Stonehuts are not built by free men.

Warriors?   Do they scream in death
When the hatchet cuts their breath?

How can cowards drive us hence?
Are they worse than pestilence?

Are they worse than skulking red men,
Ay, than restless ghosts of dead men?

Scalps—behold them! Guards be they
From the sprites of those we slay;

Holding these, we need not fear
Though their bloody wraiths appear.

Indian towns when guarded well
Never yet to stranger fell.

But if sloth shall seal our eyes
Foemen may the land surprise.

Why then wait we? Past the hills
Grow the trees that cure our ills.

Warriors, if ye tremble, follow
Northward through the river's hollow;

Westward I, the child of sun,
Lead you till our lives are done;

Waters mightier, forests vast,
Full of game we'll meet at last

So may white men vengeance minded,
By the desolate seacoast blinded,

Deem us vanished, and so daunted
At our rivers spirit-haunted

Back may get them to their home
While through sunset-lands we roam.

Warriors, let us quit the sea,
Westward, westward march with me!

———

THE DISPERSION OF THE NATION.

Mad wind! mad wind off the sea!
Indian nations, trembling, flee—

Gray wolves! gray wolves overhead!
Northward by old Hudson's bed.

Where the Mohawk cuts her banks,
One tribe dropped from out the ranks.

Burning war canoes that brave
Ocean's salt and giant wave,

Then the sun-chief's mighty band
Westward bore across the land.

Next, another thee preferred,
Blue Oneida, deep, unstirred!

Onondagas held the mountains,
Moors and forests, springs and fountains,

By Cayuga's blooming shore
Pitched their lodges one tribe more.

When, like moon above the earth
Peeped the lake of ocean's girth,

When the sweet sea burst in view,
Mighty Senecas withdrew.

Where a boiling water runs
Toward the land of six-moon suns,

11

And a whole sea from the rock
Tumbles sheer with awful shock—

Tuscaroras, Alleghanies!
Settled in your town each clan is.

At the last the remnant stood
Where the Father of Waters' flood

Splits the east land from the west.
There upon the chief's behest

Bridge o'er yellow waves they cast;—
When it broke, the half were past.

Shawnees, Cherokees to eastward,
The Dakotas to the westward.

Thus the Indians dwelt, the day
White men found Manhattan Bay.

Hear me! I have told you why
Indians fear the white man's eye.

THE FATE OF THE WHITE.

Mad wind! mad wind off the sea!
Tons of cloud before it flee.

Gray wolves! gray wolves overhead!
Hudson writhes within her bed.

Black, black the Palisades!
Fir-trees bow like willow blades.

White men, white men, by this token
Ye shall fly with panic broken.

Six crow's ages shall have passed
(Thrice will crows a man outlast)

White race in its turn shall blunder,
Sailing eastward, burn and plunder;

Sailing westward, it shall know
Vengeance from a mightier foe.

Proud with riches, strength and wit,
Whites will never quiet sit

Till a foeman now unknown,
Silently to manhood grown,

Whelm the boasters with a tide
Half of blood and blackness dyed.

See the gray ghosts in the cloud :
White men in their burial shroud !

Watch the terror, watch the anguish.
Children weep and women languish.

Boast your magic ; live your day
Indians, white men pass away.

THE TWO GIANTS.

THE TWO GIANTS.

1876.

LAPPED within two mighty seas,
Washed by stream and dried with breeze,
Throbbing with mysterious motions
Of the airs and of the oceans,
Lie two giants, man and woman,
Continental, superhuman;
They have read in waking dreams
By flashes vast of starry beams
One day more on rolling spheres
Where mortals spell a hundred years.

First the dauntless Genovese
Stirred them from a slumberous ease.
Next day with the Puritan
Through the mangod vigor ran.

Celt and Frank and Cavalier
Gave him hope and liberal cheer;
Still a day, whose close we bless,—
And giant and dark giantess
Willed their sinewy backs be free
And burst the gyves of tyranny.

On this fourth day's glorious eve
They must freedom full achieve
From pupilage, a tyrant's name,
Faults that even giants lame,
Ignorance and greed of pelf,
Overweening pride of self,
Lust of conquest, luxuries,
All ignoble slaveries,—
Ready so, with open grace,
To look the wide world in the face.

By deathless camp-fires of the sun
Round about the earth that run
Half-reclining, vast they lie
Separate beneath the sky.
Warm are knees and mighty thighs,
Cool their bodies huge in size;

Winds of autumn gently fan
Breasts of woman and of man ;
While their foreheads clear and cold
Well to north and southward hold.

I.

Close against the line of light
Where are even day and night
In her skirt of forests sweet
SHE has curled her languid feet.
Flash with white and yellow ore
Dimpled knees in Ecquador,
While her mighty virgin zone
Lies along the Amazon.
There she rests, her dreamy eyes
Lit with scorn and fierce surprise
When she feels the restless blaze
Of the northern giant's gaze;
Will not note his glances bold
But, coucht soft in careless fold
Of her silk-bark kirtle, white
'Gainst her eyes of blue midnight,

11*

Her musky side supporting still
On the mountains of Brazil
And breathing spices soporific
Blown across the South Pacific,
Ponders on the fading gray
Westward over Chiloé.

She would sound the happy past;
Future's smile she will not see.
Careless, tawny hands are cast
Up behind the symmetry
Of her dark head throned in state
O'er the land of River Plate;
Spread her locks along the strand
Of dripping pines in Fireland
While the soft-wing'd memories stir
Through that antique mind of her.

She has been a glorious queen;
Wars and empires she has seen
Drop like plummets loosed from line
Into space without confine.
With her old force ever young
She would resurrect her dead
Hear what bard or Inca sung,

Ask them why they all are fled;
Runes in knotted cords unravel,
Lichen-eaten sculptures read,
Sift the secret-heaping gravel
Where her marvelous rivers speed;
Con the lore of eldest East,
The meanings lost of mystic feast,
And seek a clew to all the haste
Pulsing faster from the West;
Summon up the shades of old,
Monarchs and her champions bold;
Rend their graves and cry to them
Westward march of men to stem.
She to savage war would harden
Myriad hands on fertile plain;
She would marshal once again
The tillers of her tropic garden
So to guard untouched her honor
From the giant gazing on her.

II.

From his eyes of glittering lakes
HE the mist of morning shakes;

From the white gates of the dawn
Now his watchful gaze is drawn.
Filled with new-grown energy
Born beyond the eastern sea
And with knotted muscles swelling
With the fresh life in him welling,
He, his awful head upreared,
Plants his fist below his beard
While a thought serene and tender
Mingles with his blue eye's splendor
And his forehead white with snows
Ruddy with his passion grows.

Southward fall his glances quick
As a cloud of javelins thick,
And his restless spirit trembles
Toward the woman, who dissembles,
Conscious that the spell which flows
From her seeming-deep repose
Fiery though his being goes.
Small his skill to play a part;
Yet his veins, replete with longing,
Fill the caverns of his heart,
Till the organ tones come thronging

So enormous deep and slow
That mortals fancy north winds blow :—

III.

" Virgin of the eldest eld,
Young, mysteriously fair,
Long enough have you withheld
Kiss of bridegroom from your hair.
Not as oft before do I
Rudely grasp that sacred zone
But with chaste sobriety
Come to plead with love alone.
While your slumber of despair
Scarce by islander was broke
And to keener life you were
Scarce by Asian seer awoke,
While the planets sang in choir
How the great through toil aspire
My strong spirit left our fire.

" Marched with myriad, slaying men
My quick soul on Asian plain,
India and the Ukraine harried,
Vigor new to Syria carried,

Russia swept and laid in Greece
Beauty's seed to bloom in peace.
My soul Kymric battles won;
I was burned in Babylon;
Blasting culture, forced in turn
Culture from the wreck to learn,
I in legions of old Rome
Served, and overthrew my home.
Of victory the thousand ills,
Crime and famine, pestilence,
War that slays and peace that kills,
Glut of pride and brutish sense
Still defeated and oppressed me
Till upon our pristine hearth
After circuit of the earth
Now my soul has repossessed me.

" Virgin of the spirit shy,
You that like the llama fly
Lovely eyed still higher, higher
To the sharp crags of your ire,
You must learn your hates to rhyme
With this renovating time.

Have you asked yourself the meaning
Of your body's northward leaning?
Winds and secret currents bear
My blood southward toward your feet;
Do you drop no hidden tear
For the one you long to meet
Who should rouse you from your dream,
Read for you the future clear,
Tell what is and what doth seem
What is far and what is near—
Who should make your languid veins
Thrill with better life and new,
Lead you queen in mutual chains
Of the wise, the good, the true?

"Virgin of the mighty past
·I, of modern things the last,
Love you with a constant passion
Such as northlands only fashion.
I the north adore the south;
Heart to heart and mouth to mouth
Each shall be an equal lover,
Each the other's weakness cover!

Do not scorn the restless West,
Ponder well my bold request;
Here I cite you, dreamy East,
To our joyful wedding feast!
Virgin great, no longer fly me,
But in honor trust and try me!"

IV.

Thus the giant, half upreared,
Utters through his curling beard
Sounds so wavewide to that woman
That they pass the senses human;
Only here and there a word
On mountain-tops by prophets heard
Brings the mortal's heart to mouth
With love for all the glorious South;
Leaping down, he pipes again
Peace and brotherhood to men.

But the brooding ocean's daughter
Answers him not who besought her,
Yet she listens while the rays
Of his eyes like sunshafts blaze

Into hers.   She does not mock
When their glances interlock.
Even as when day is done
Moon still sees the face of sun
Shine her eyes with luring light,
Torches toward the bridal night.
Love so earnest well may guess
In the no a lurking yes.
Smiles can quench the rising sneer;
Lo, she quakes—the time is near
For dreamy East and martial West
To sink upon each other's breast.

HESPERUS.

HESPERUS.

Do ye perceive, shapes of the western skies,
Apart from joy such as to life belongs,
Know ye, O maryelous fabrics, when the eyes
Of mortals watch ye, how their ears yearn for songs?
　　Slow-chanted poems, changing in form and hue,
Are ye aware of wide symphonic moves
Among your star-crowned pinnacles? and you,
Ye sea-foam strips at mid-day—gullies, grooves,
　　Fantastic turrets, bastions and holy fanes,
Cities scarce built when ruined, do ye reckon
How to the heart of man your mysteries beckon,
What of your glories in man's soul remains?

　　Or is this sky a dome of polished blue,
A crystal-pillared chapel on whose walls
Some humorous mighty power doth still endue
A pageant-travesty of all that crawls

About the earth-crust?   From the infant's crow,
From laughter of a little red-cheeked boy
To shocks of armies and the overthrow
Of century-mortised cities; from the joy
   Of still-voiced grasses to the angry blare
Of hurricanes and earthquakes,—each great text,
Plain to high souls whom envy never vexed,—
Folly, crime, love and wisdom, all are there.

Then, how that boundless vast artificer
Must love to shift his scenes from dawn to dawn;
To breathe in curves exquisite, subtly drawn,
With delicate tints and angels' pinion-stir,
   Some hint of earthly happiness or woe!
Perchance a bridal or a funeral train
Or thoughts that scud across a maddened brain
When hope looks true and all the pulses glow;
   Perchance unsounded problems of the world,
A law, a truth, a virtue elemental,
A hieroglyphic close-wrapped, transcendental,
Never by man's dull wit to be unfurled!

From off this sheer and skyward promontory
I see a bay where meet the converg'd lines
Of Western traffic and behold the glory
That from a nation in yon city shines.
　Still, there be promptings, secret calls that turn
Westward my face, though the night's end may glow
Fair with false sunrise, high though the mid-sun burn,
Though evening's gale the sunset caldron blow:
　Why in that core flamboyant must I gaze
Longing to march westward, ah, far away?
Why do our souls, seeking a cloud-Cathay,
Run toward the sun along those glittering ways?

　Say we are waves, urged by a devious current
Obedient to mysterious laws of mass,
Never for all our boasts to be aberrant
From the vast Plan through which all comes to pass.
　Or, being plants fed with a quicker sap
That faster move than brethren of the meadow,
Do we lean after, out of night's dark lap,
Afraid to brave the round earth's starlit shadow?
　Or are we poured like Norway's living flood?—
O'er crag and lake the myriad-breeding lemming

Moves with an instinct that will bear no stemming
Till the Atlantic drowns the prodigious brood.

Once did the West contain those blessed islands
The ancients fabled?　The red Indians know
Moored in the evening sky, their happy highlands
Where the pale foeman flies the exultant bow.
　Perhaps our home was once a golden region
Long sunk beneath the sinister gray sea,
And that is why a world-wide dim religion
Motions men on to where that land may be;
　Perhaps beneath the treacherous Atlantic
It slumbers now, while through the oozy ways
The starfish creeps; in palaces gigantic
House mighty sharks and human-visaged rays.

Or is it memory?　If from twilight ages
Our ancestors have westward, westward marched,
Broken through all, fought, and by deadly stages
Mastered seas, sands, wind-rent, by deserts parched,
　Then may they, many a time, in separate æons,

Have stood just here, noting with savage gladness
In blood-red skies, loud gales where all is sadness,
Signs of their prey, and heard triumphant pæans;
 Till, following ever on the ancient trail,
A thousand times girdling the pied earth's rind. . .
Could it be they, whose dim foredeeds avail
To urge us westward with this longing blind?

 But if this height full many a time was trod
By antique men facing the beckoning west,
Were there not some whose naked feet were shod
With wings ideal?—on whose dull hairy breast
 Weighed all this life-long misery of a crawling?
Who sighed for change and in each coarse limb
  yearned,
For wind, for space, for more light dumbly calling—
Watching the stars, proudly the flat earth spurned?
 Such if there were, like to an ant with wings
That soars scarce once, but, being hatched in the
  mud,
Hastes to the earth and off her pinions flings,
Back they did plunge, ay, back to the old wildwood!

12

How many æons more? Shall thousand races
Like individuals live, die, wake and sleep?
Once more a thousand times shall all the faces
Of earth perceive the human myriads creep,
    Before man's shoulders have put forth their wings,
Before man's brain, remembering and forgetting—
Pure force the senses are no more besetting—
Shall grow to a bird that without discord sings?
    Why, the old Gauls esteemed this frame a raiment
Round deathless souls, and the brave heathen loaned
His coin and cattle 'gainst an actual payment
In some new land beyond his burial mound!

    What if it now were true? The dull earth spurning
Perhaps we too while gazing on yon gold
Shall through these eyes behold the red sky turning
To gray and know our last day by has rolled;
    Then when the body will no more obey,
Why shall we not—a mist, a shade, a thought—
Finding death's pruning-knife great fruit has brought,
Wing westward still after the flying day?
    We may not speak to mortal friends or foes,
Nor shall we care so to infringe that Plan:

Mysteries obscure and wonders we shall scan
Wrapped in divine, ineffable repose.

Are not the pleasures of the growing boy
Thrice those of infants? and when mind gains sway
O'er matter does not an intenser joy
Break on the student as the kneaded clay
Of his five wits grows finer in the straining?
So at the last, when in the slow machine
Of brain and body there's no heat remaining,
Shall not the engineer desert the scene?
O, to sweep on across the windy mountains,
Study all lands, oceans and woods and airs,
Search every river to its tiny fountains,
Track men of guile through their fine-spun affairs!

Deaf to its roar are those who make their home
Where sheer Niagara jars the primeval rock.
Let them but go and come: the awful boom
Strikes on their new-born ears with thunderous shock!
Blind are these eyes, except they note some
    change—

They cannot see, until by contrasts taught;
Then how obtuse, how narrow in their range
Are human senses and is human thought!
    But,—when the trammels fall! what sights, sounds,
        tastes,
Globed in our perfect and unfettered minds,
Shall greet us then!   Silent and moveless wastes
May sound with anthems mightier than the wind's.

What time the mullein, rising from her ashes,
Builds from the dry heart of her crumpled leaves
A gold-tipped campanilé till it flashes
Like the famed bird that, dying, life receives—
    Then to review the scenes of earthly bliss!
To launch in thought again upon the stream
Of summery passion, where the sigh and kiss
Each other's sweetness to enhance did seem—
    Kiss like those fresh gold blossoms, and the sigh
Like this brown wreath of winter-bitten leaves:—
Shall we not smile, rehearsing words gone by,
Wise, far too wise, to dwell on that which grieves?

Some one foreknew the desperate heart of man
When stars and moon and the bright northern sky,
Obedient to a Sun-of-suns, began
Through the dark night the name of Light to cry:
    A fly's love-lantern to the swamp is pledge
That somewhere dwells a midmost soul of flame;
Through the black storm a sword of dazzling edge
Flashes a hope and scores an eternal name:
    And since the night forms but a lovely version
Of glorious day, different but no less real—
Mortal, look up! so shall this clay's dispersion
Prove but the step into a life ideal.

Through the courtesy of the editors of Lippincott's and Scribner's Magazines, and of The Penn Monthly, some of these poems are now reprinted. The greater part appear for the first time.

TABLE OF CONTENTS.

Lightning Source UK Ltd.
Milton Keynes UK
UKHW020923011218
333087UK00009B/1225/P